LETS GO Query

I0015238

The AS/400 & IBM i Pocket Query Guide

QuikCourse: Query/400 By Example

by Brian W. Kelly

– A Comprehensive Book of Query/400 examples & information for the new Query User –

This book is based on Query/400 and the QuikCourse™ classroom education modules.

LETS GO PUBLISH

Contains significant reference material, how-to's, and insightful tutorials.

The AS/400 & IBM I Pocket Query Guide
Author Brian W. Kelly
"I learn more about technology when after a year or two, I re-read one of my own books. It is amazing what we take for granted!
This book is very similar to the 2006 version with changes in readability and some function additions.

Published by: LETS GO PUBLISH!
Brian P. Kelly, Publisher
P.O Box 621
Wilkes-Barre PA 18703
www.letsgopublish.com
Original book was edited by Jessica Webb
Library of Congress Copyright Information Pending
ISBN # **978-0-9980848-8-6**

Last two publishing dates   February 2006, October 2016

10   9   8   7   6   5   4   3   2   1

Dedication

To the most popular IBM Query program of all time. Without Query/400, there would be lots of missing information in the world.

Acknowledgments

*These acknowledgments are copied from the 2006 version of this book.
An updated version of the acknowledgments is at
www.letsgopublish.com. Look for acknowledgments on left menu. Query
acknowledgments were originally written in 2002 and then updated with
the code in 2006. The acknowledgments are printed here as they existed
in 2006. As then, they are very sincere.*

*Please note that since her eminence, Wiley Ky Eyely, a recent friend of a
publishing magnate was not yet born at this time in 2006, we defer
respectfully to the online version of the acknowledgments for her
individual kudos, with full deference to Ms. Ky Eyely.*

I would like to thank many people for helping me in this effort.

I would first like to thank my immediate family, starting with my
lovely and dear wife, Patricia. Again, as I offer in all my books,
my wife Patricia is my source. She is the person who keeps me
alive and sane and well—in more ways than can be mentioned.
She is the glue that holds our whole family together. Besides
that, she keeps getting better looking as the years go by, and I
love to see her wonderful face every day in my life. Thank you
God for that!

Her daddy, a wonderful man in his own right, Smokey Piotroski,
called his little girl Packy as a nickname. Though Stash is now
with the Angels, I love that name and the person who wears it
and I still use it to address my little Packy. God gave me a gift
that keeps me going. Thank you Packy for all you do to keep me
and our whole family well and mostly, thank you for the smile
that you always put on my face.

I would also like to thank my twenty-one year-old daughter,
Katie, who is still my little baby doll. Kate helps me in any way
she can. Even more than that, her sweet voice and her
accomplished guitar playing gets the muse racing as my fingers

pound the keyboard. Katie is starting to feel better now and we thank God for that but it still is not easy for her. She is on her way to being OK. I thank my Katie for she will always be Daddy's Little Girl. I love you very much. A special thank you also goes to Dr. Patrick Kerrigan, the consummate physician and good friend of our family. Dr. Kerrigan is working his way up the list in record time. Dr. Patrick comes to the job with the abilities of Hippocrates and the patience of Job. He has left no stone unturned in helping Katie through her illness, and his work continues as a solution is on its way.

Thanks also go out to my twenty-four year-old son, Michael, who more than made the dean's list in his last semester at King's College this year as he received his B.S. Degree in Accounting. Michael had very good LSATs and his academic record was more than enough for him to be accepted in Law School and he will be beginning his three year trek this month. I am always happy to have my youngest son close by so I am going to miss him very much.

I also thank my twenty-five-year-old son, Brian, who edits and publishes many of my books. He is an astute grammarian and a prolific writer in his own right. He just knocked 'em dead recently in Law School and graduated Magna Cum Laude.

Brian spent a few months taking courses in preparation for the Bar Examination, which he passed no sweat on the first try. After a short break, Brian will be starting a clerkship. Congratulations Brian, you make us very proud. Mom and I are very proud of all of our children and we thank each of them for their work in academia and their efforts on our behalf.

Thanks also to the extended family who are always there to lend a helping hand. Barb, Kim & Dave, Dawn, Cindy & Dave Boyle, Megan and Sean are some of the most wonderful family in my life. And dad Joe, with the angels, always gets his plugs in. Thanks also to Melissa and Paul Sabol and their new baby boy Paul IV. Crocodile Dundee Sabol and the Plains Police

Department are always there to make sure all the families are safe.

Accomplishments often materialize because of a strong friendship infrastructure. I am pleased to have a number of great friends. Among them is my longtime best friend Dennis Grimes, who is always there to help, though he may think everything I write sounds the same. Professor Grimes is on the faculty with me at Marywood University and he is a CIO for Klein Wholesale.

He is very talented and very helpful. Many of his quips and quotes find their way into my writing. Barbara Grimes, Patricia Grimes Yencha, Elizabeth (Wizzler), Mary the PhD., Denyse back from the U.K., Grandma Viola, and Grandma Gert also pitch in whenever the opportunity arises. Dennis helps me in whatever way I ask, especially when I am stuck. I really appreciate all you do for me "D." Thank you

The busiest guy on all of my book projects, besides myself, has always been Joe McDonald. Joe is the businessman in our publishing venture, and in that, he's all business. Joe is the former Publisher of the Scranton Tribune/Scrantonian Newspaper. So he's got the right background to make sure everything is A-OK! Our next book is not going to be technical as we are moving the publishing business to include children's books and third party authors.

Joe assures me that after this book's second printing, he will have the courage to lead me to the children's side of the business where our next book is scheduled to be The Adventures of Eddy (The Dog) written by Joe's Grandson. Soon, it will be on the bookshelves of America. My thanks also go to Peg McDonald for making sure that Joe is always ready for action.

Of course, the long list of helping hands contains lots of names: Gerry Rodski and his wonderful friend-- Joyce, Jeanne and Farmer Joe Elinsky, John and Carol Anstett, Grandma Leona and Grandma Annie (from Mayflower), Carolyn and Joe

Langan, Bob & Cathy Wood, Karen and Al Komorek (Al was alive when this was written originally], Joe and Betta Demmick, Bonnie and George Mohanco, Becker and Robin Mohanco, Lilya, Josh, and Alaina Like Mohanco, Bob and Nettie Lussi, Kim and Ruth Borland--- they are all there when needed..

Other helping hands include Dr. Lou and Marie Guarnieri as well as Mary and Cindy Guarnieri, whose hands have been indispensable. I can't forget Mike and Frannie Kurilla & Frankie and Tony, Jerry and Hedy Cybulski, Linda DeBoo and Bob Buynak, Joe, the Chief, LaSarge, John and Susan Rose, and Dave and Nancy Books. Thanks also to Dr. Rex Dumdum from Marywood-- my academic mentor. Special thanks also to the E.L. Meyers Class of 1965 (40th reunion last year) for some early training in the art of writing.

And don't let me forget Patricia's parents, Arline and Stanley Piotroski, who continue to guide us in our lives. Cathy and Marty Piotroski, Dr. Susan Piotroski and Dr. Mitch Bornstein, Matt and Allie, Dr. Stan Piotroski, Carol Piotroski, Sister Marlene, Justin and Katie, Merek, MacKenzie, Myranda, Erin, Ralph Harvey, Lynn, and Scott Piotroski, Pierre Le Kep. The Kelly parents -- Ed and Irene also provide guidance from upstairs as well as direct intervention as needed; Anna Maye, Nancy and Angel Jim Flannery (Leland (No K) Zard), Renee (Bean), Jimmy (Jim Bob), Bridget, Mary (MeeWee), Danny, Michael (McPike) , Ken (La Rue), Jen, Angel David Davidow (Brunoch Zard), Stephen (P.Q. Whoozer), Matthew(M.Q. Peph), Bailee Roo, Viva La Vieve, and Billiard Peph, Joe and Rosalee, Raymond, Paula, and the real Sparkey. Mary and Bill Daniels, Liz (Weezler), Bri, Megan (Megeldeebaigledee), Bill Jr (Billdog) ., Vicky, Sophia (Chubby Cheeks,) Elise (La Leese), Diane and Joe Kelly, Tara and Col, Ed and Eudart Kelly, Eddie, John, and Robert. Bill Rolland- Notre Dame's # 1 Fan and master of accommodations, Bill Kustas, Bill & Helen Kush, Steve and Shelly Bartolomei, Keith and Dorie Zinn, Cheryl Danowski, Ricky, Joane, Briana and Eric Bayer, Rick and Donna Pinkofski, and of course the great musical cutter Harrison Arthur and his friend Harry Heck Jr. More thanks to Judy Jones and Jerry Reisch and Judy Judy Judy Seroska.

[I know I have corrected many of the acknowledgement mistakes since this book was printed but this is the original. For the updates, please go to www.letsgopublish.com]

Going back to the top of the list of helpers is my wonderful and huge pack of cousins. The list begins with the Uncles and Aunts, many of whom are now Angels. Uncle Nick and Aunt Emma McKeown, Dave and Kathleen Conklin, Rita and Frank DeRiancho, Joan and Tom Nelson, Aunt Ruth and Uncle Joe McKeown, Kathy and Joe McKeown Jr., Aunt Louise and Uncle Jimmy McKeown, Patsy, Danny and Jerry McKeown, Nina and Jim Brady, Jimmy Brady, Tommy and Mary Rowan, Arlene and Richard May, Little Tommy Rowan, Helen and Joe Drexinger, and all the other cousins, uncles & aunts who can't make it to the special muse event every summer in Montrose.

Of course, there's Uncle Johnny Kelly, Aunt Catherine and Leonard Lamascola, Aunt Mary Kelly, Sharon, Maureen, Jud, Pat Jr., and Tommy Kelly. Red Cloud is also on the list for his due diligence in writing postcards.

In the special care category, Dr. Lou has been making sure that my bones are aligned properly for years. So that I can give those speeches with a bright smile, I got some big help from Dr. Lou Kicha the Great and his highly competent team of professionals at Aspen Dental-- John Cicon, Carol Kephart, Nicole Arnone, Anita Florek, and the tooth architect, Mary Lou Lennox. Thank you all very much.

Special acknowledgments to Steven Dressler and Howard Klein, the top management team at Klein Wholesale Distributors in Wilkes-Barre, PA, who use Query to the fullest. Their vision, foresight, and execution have brought Klein to the enviable position of being the third largest candy and tobacco wholesaler in the United States.

Various members of the Klein development staff offered information over the time in which this book was written. In alphabetical order, by first name, the Klein team includes: Barb Chaderton, Bill 'Curly' Kepics, Cindy Dorzinsky, Cindy Goodwin, Dennis Grimes, Eric Priest, Jeff Massaker, Jerry Reisch, Joe Byorick, Joe Rydzewski, John Robbins, Paula Terpak, Rod Smith, and Rosalind Robertson.

I would also like to thank Nancy Lavan, our sponsor at Offset Paperback, our printer [who guided all publishing efforts though we have chosen CreateSpace for this update.] She continually encourages us in our writing and publishing efforts. Chris Grieves, our new customer service person has made working with the printing process an easy task. Special thanks go to Michele Thomas, who takes ideas and makes wonderful images from them, such as this wonderful cover.

To sum up my acknowledgments, as I do in every book that I have written, I am compelled to offer that I am truly convinced that "the only thing you can do alone in life is fail." Thanks to my family, good friends, and a helping team, I was not alone.

Table of Contents

Preface:

This pocket guide introduces the most popular Query package for any IBM computer to the AS/400 and IBM i community. Though it is designed for non-computer experts, this guide can also be a powerful teaching / learning tool for AS/400 and non-AS/400 computer technicians who have minimal familiarity with the Query/400 product

Since all information starts with data access, this book is designed to help you get information from your database with a minimum of pain and effort. It is built specifically from an AS/400 and IBM i computer user's perspective. To help jump start the process, it comes with a comprehensive set of exercises as well as a succinct and pithy primer on the popular database that is integrated with the AS/400 and iSeries (now shortened to DB2/400).

Rather than bore you with long lists of facts about the query program, after a brief introduction, the book takes on a case study approach. This is just the ticket for the user community to easily embrace this work.

Once you are on your way, you won't want this pocket guide to be far from your pockets. We start with a few short introductory chapters to bring you up to speed on the facilities within Query/400. Before you know it, you are in the middle of building and running your own Queries.

Every menu option in Query is covered with extensive treatment in the very important results field and select records areas. There's an example for just about any result field that you have to build and for every record you have to select. In fact, most of the time, you'll find more than one example to help you learn even better and sooner than otherwise.

The case study moves through every single menu option of the Query/400 utility program – even the elusive notion of collating sequence. After each case study menu option is completed, we don't stop there. Example after example are explored and explained so that you get the full Query treatment, not just the requirements of the case study.

The Query user community will enjoy the easy to read, down home style of this pocket guide. A general notion of how your files are structured will get you going. To help you in this effort, we have included a database primer for Query/400. This can help you gain familiarity with some of the terms your IT people may throw around in their discussions with you. This primer demystifies the database and helps make it your friend.

Remember, there are no instant experts in anything. This is true also for Query/400. However, with the combination of the simplicity and richness of the Query/400 product and this Query pocket guide, you can become an almost-expert in a reasonably short period of time. This book can sure help you get pointed in the right direction and help you hang on for your ultimate success.

Programmers and other developers who do not have extensive Query/400 skills will find this guide especially useful in coming up to speed very quickly. There are literally tons of screen captures along with simple explanations for what otherwise would be a difficult area of study.

Technical people are not particularly interested in tough reading books and stilted manuals to learn valuable tools and techniques. This book is easy to read and right on target for the future Query User and the programming community. You won't want to put it down. It will help you immediately.

Because there are so many screen captures as you walk through the case study, you will find that you may not even need a machine to gain from the case studies. The tutorial-like style makes it seem as if you are on your AS/400 doing the work. Therefore, this pocket guide to Query/400 works well in your favorite reading room, wherever it may be, with no machine involvement.

However, it also works well right from your AS/400 or IBM i workstation as you go through these exercises on your favorite AS/400 or IBM i based system. The test files are downloadable from the Web (www.letsgopublish.com) and are easily installed on your AS/400 to save you work.

Though it may take a bit more than 24 hours for you to be running the likes of Join Queries, you may actually be able to do it in less. You certainly will get the idea of how to get a Query completed regardless of the task or the output distribution.

If you are an IT person, there is nothing to fear in learning Query/400. Knowing how to Query does not mean you will be doing Queries for others your whole technical life. However, it can certainly save you a lot of programming time when the answer is available in five minutes with Query. Moreover, it can help you in your application testing as you get reports about key database value changes in the update type applications you may be writing.

This Query/400 QuikCourse is designed to make it easy for you to learn the native AS/400 and iSeries Query program. There is only one Query/400.

As a Query QuikCourse, this module originally was a one-day standup formal classroom course. It was designed with slides and notes for stand-up instruction. This book is the direct result of its conversion to a stand-alone lecture / tutorial / reference format with plenty of action and plenty of examples.

Yes, you can learn Query/400 just by reading this book. All of the material from the Query/400 course is in here, plus there is a database primer and a glossary that has been loaded to the web for easy downloading. There is no CD since the practice databases are already available on the Web.

Go ahead and leaf through this book now. You'll see it is chocked full of examples - one example after another. That's how most people learn. Again, many screen shots are included so you can play right along with your AS/400 or IBM i system.

Who Should Read this book?

New programmers, some existing programmers, supervisors, operation personnel, and end users should all take this overgrown QuikCourse.

There are plenty of smart PC technicians running around in every business and institution. Most of these folks could catch on to Query/400 very quickly with the help of this pocket guide. They too, would appreciate the opportunity to learn Query/400 and could serve the company well in assuring that user departments are self-sufficient in their use of Query/400. This book may be all you need to move them off the mark.

If as the IT Director, you have always wanted to be able to tell your team what you know about Query/400 on the AS/400 and iSeries, but you did not have the time, I've done it for you. I've said what you would have said if you had the time to say it Moreover, the folks at LETS GO PUBLISH think you'll like what you would have said.

We wish you well in your Query endeavors, and we hope to see you again reading other LETS GO PUBLISH offerings.

Brian W. Kelly
Wilkes-Barre, Pennsylvania

About the Author

Brian W. Kelly is a retired Assistant Professor in the Business Information Technology (BIT) program at Marywood University, where he also served as the IBM i and midrange systems technical advisor to the IT faculty. Kelly developed and taught many college and professional courses in the IT and business areas. He is also a contributing technical editor to IT Jungle's "The Four Hundred" and "Four Hundred Guru" Newsletters.

A former IBM Senior Systems Engineer, he has an active consultancy in the information technology field, (www.kellyconsulting.com). He is the author of 87 books and numerous articles (hundreds) about current IT topics. Kelly is a frequent speaker at COMMON, IBM conferences, and other technical conferences and user group meetings across the United States. His favorite COMMON speaker was his buddy, the late Al Barsa Jr., one of the best ever.

Though much of this book was conceived and some of it was published before today, publishing standards groups acknowledge this as Brian Kelly's 87th book. Thank you for the great support of Kelly's technical books from IT Jungle, MC Press, 29th Street Press and many seminars over the years.

I think Brian looks lots younger than 68. Don't you think?

Chapter 1 What Is AS/400 and IBM i Query?

What Is a "Query?"

IBM says that "Query is a utility that allows principals, programmers, secretaries, and other office personnel to interactively define, manage, and execute queries."

In its most simplistic form, a query is a question or an inquiry about someone or something to someone or something. The expected result of a query is an answer. When we ask a question, we are performing a query.

However, the word query, is most often thought of as a noun that reflects a question that is often required to be expressed in a formal way. Though technically, informal questions can be called queries, the word is typically associated with a more formal process. As many English words, it comes from the Latin quaere, which is the imperative form of quaerere, meaning to ask or seek.

Query with Computers

In the 1970's as more and more valuable information began to be stored on computer systems, the information science community formalized the term to mean a request for information. As relational database systems began to be deployed on computer systems in the 1980's, the term query took on the meaning of a formal request to a database. At this time, the Structured Query language or SQL, became the favorite computer language of computer professionals.

(A database is a collection of facts, about business entities, organized and stored on hard disks. Employee data is an example.)

Query the Internet

In the mid 1990's as the Internet and its many search engines became more the norm than the exception, the term query took on another, yet similar meaning. It was expanded to mean a formal request to a database or search engine. When employed with a search engine, the user expects to receive back an answer representing a number of potential "hits." From these "hits," the user can surf the answer set to find the most applicable to the search criteria. When deployed with a database for data retrieval purposes, the user expects to receive back an answer representing the database records that match the search criteria.

Checking out IBM's Word

Now, let's make some more sense of the Query product that we are studying, from IBM's words: "Query is a utility that allows principals, programmers, secretaries, and other office personnel to interactively define, manage, and execute queries."

A utility is a pre-written program that helps provide value to a computer system. The Query utility can help just about everybody in a business organization to build and run queries. In other words, it guides you through a process so that you can ask your formal question within its rules so that you have a good chance of getting a correct answer.

Define Queries

The Query utility forces you to tell it about the database files you want to examine and then it helps you pick the data elements you want to see. It then helps you define totals and summary breaks and shape a report to meet your needs. You do this interactively with the Query utility. This means that you do something, then the computer does something and together you get through the process until you have formally asked your question. The result of this is called a query definition (QRYDFN).

Managing Queries

Because it may take a few minutes or more to define a query, IBM lets you name your definitions and save them for later use. For example, you might have a query named BILLING to see what you have billed in a day, and you might have a Query named HR for an employee listing. You might even have some queries that you want to delete or copy for other people to use. This is known as managing your queries.

Executing Queries

The last part of a Query session is running your query. During the definition, you will have chosen to send the query results to one of three places: 1.) a new database so that you can email it to somebody, or you can keep the results indefinitely, or 2.) the display from which you are working, or 3.) a printed report for later viewing.

When you finish your definition and save your query, you can then run your query. Based on your output selection, the result is will appear in any of the three forms as noted above. The computer term for running your queries after they are defined is *Executing Queries*. However, most users prefer the term *Running Queries*.

IBM's Query utility therefore helps you ask the questions you need answered; helps you remember the specific questions you ask; and then goes and gets you the answers you have requested. Of course, if after all the help IBM gives in forming your question, you ask it improperly, such as asking for all the men instead of all the women in an employee listing, there is no guarantee by IBM or anybody else that your question will generate a correct answer.

Overview

Query/400 is menu-driven and it gives you a measure of control over what data is selected, as well as the shape of the final report output. For example you can send any query to a display, a report (printer), or a database file.

Programmers often use Query/400's database output facility to build intermediate results for long, complex queries or to produce files which are more usable for end user queries. In essence, they use the Query program as an extraction vehicle to build a mini data warehouse.

The database receives the full field definitions from the based on files. Therefore the output is as usable as any other AS/400 database file and can be used for any purpose. Before IBM pulled the plug on its OfficeVision/400, the product linked to Query/400 which provided the selection records for text-data merge.

Uses Integrated Database

As an information tool, AS/400 Query is a decision support utility which can be used to gain information from the AS/400 data bases. For Example, you can obtain information from any files that have been defined on the system using the following methods:

1. Data description specifications (DDS),
2. Interactive data definition utility (IDDU)
3. Structured Query Language (SQL)

Raison D'etre

 Just like everything else, Query/400 has a reason for being. Query is used most often when your application code does not provide the reporting necessary for requests, but the data is available in the production database. Since no package is complete, and no custom design can hope to define and satisfy all of the information needs of

an organization, a strong Query package is necessary to fill in the holes.
Query can be used to:

1. Select
2. Arrange (sort and/or summarize),
3. Analyze

It operates upon data stored in one or more data base files. It is used to produce reports and/or other data files which can be displayed or printed. Queries can be built against any or many database files.

Query Versatility

Query provides a level of versatility that is not found in standard reporting. With the product, you can perform the following tasks:

1. Create your own queries
2. Store them by name for later recall
3. Run them once or as often as you like
4. Run other queries you did not create
5. Run a default query against a data base file.

Original Purpose

When IBM originally designed, the Query product, which is used on AS/400 and iSeries, the target audience was the System/36 user. The Sytem/36 shop was characterized with typically having very few computer literate personnel on staff, available to work with the system. Thus it was important for IBM to build ease-of-use features into the product, since the shops could not afford to hire professional data analysts and programmers. The result was System/36 Query, which became the design building block for the AS/400 Query product, you use today.

Ease-Of-Use

The ease-of-use features, incorporated into the Query/400 product, include the following:

1.   Fully menu guided process.

2.   Online, cursor sensitive help available for every option.

3.   Prototype execution during definition to extract results quickly.

4.   Work with lists facilities enables selection from:
-       A.   A list of files
-       B.   A list of libraries

5.   Fast path definition.

6.   Menu bypass — select options for specific needs.

Pre-Built Queries

In addition to being able to build queries, the product also provides commands for you to run pre-built queries. For example, the RUNQRY (Run Query) command can be executed from a menu, from an interactive command line, or from a CL Program.

Since the AS/400 comes with an integrated database, there are no special commands needed to bring data into the Query/400 environment. AS/400 database file objects are supported and no import/export is required to use them. The RUNQRY command works with definitions that were previously saved during the Query build process. This enables professionals or programmers to build specific queries that users with little or no query experience can easily run.

Interactive or Batch?

All queries, whether defined on the fly or pre-built, can run in either the interactive or batch modes. In today's modern iSeries boxes it is typically better for users to submit their queries for batch execution than it is to execute them from the interactive panels. Without getting too technical the reason for this is that IBM taxes work that is not submitted and there is no performance tax (penalty) for work that is submitted to batch.

Using Queries on Other Machines

When queries are executing, they do not require the Query product, since the Query extraction facilities are built right into the operating system.

So, now that we have some knowledge about the general facilities and ease-of-use capabilities of the AS/400 Query product, let's see what other capabilities the product may have besides basic list and database creation.

Advanced Query Capabilities

AS/400 Query has a number of advanced capabilities built into the product. For example, it has a comprehensive record join capability with up to 32 data base files. In the formation of the joined query result, the product supports multiple join types and up to 100 join tests.

You can also use joined logical files in your queries. However, you must be careful since the maximum number of files in a Query is 32. Using a joined logical file does not increase the number of files that are permitted in a Query.

Since joined logical files have at least two and can have up to 32 dependent physical files, the number of files defined to Query/400 will always be less than 32 when there is at least one joined file defined. As an extreme example, if you were to use one logical file definition with 32 underlying physical files in your Query, you would be out of files. Even though just one file were defined, 32 files would actually be part of the Query. Thus, you would be at the maximum file definitions.

Query Join Support

The various forms of the Join supported include the following:

1.   Select records with matching records in all the joined files

2.   Select all primaries and include all matched secondaries

3.   Select only the primaries with one or more unmatched secondaries and all the secondary records which also match the unselected primaries

User Defined Fields

Query also provides the ability for you to define up to 100 result fields which are not in the database and then to sort on those fields to better facilitate reporting. The fields can be numeric or character in nature.

Field Selection and Field Ordering

Query excels in two additional areas - field selection and field ordering. Suppose you have one or several humongous databases consisting of well over 500 fields. Query/400 permits up to 500 fields on a single report.

You can argue that is way more than the number of data elements one should ever want on a report. The fact is that it is a big number so that you should not run out of field room in your queries. In addition to specifying the fields, you order the sequence of the fields in their appearance within your report. From the leftmost column to the rightmost column each field in a Query is assigned a numeric sequence which keeps it where it should be in the report.

When you are defining your Query, you pick you files, then you create the result fields you need. After you have all of your fields noted, from the database and those that you have defined within the query, then you can select and order up to 500 fields for a left-to-right report display.

Record Selection

After field selection and ordering, you are asked for any *record* selection criteria. This is where you assure that only the data records you want are included in your report. As in all areas, stretched from the System/36's modest capabilities, the Advanced Query Definition allow for comprehensive record selection.

Up to 100 test operations of nine different types can be used to grab just the records you want. Additionally, the report output facilities support the editing of numeric fields to make the report much more readable than relying on edit codes in the database.

Sorting Results

As you would expect, the Advanced Query Definition Options also support sorting records so that the report is displayed or printed in the desired sequence. The limits of sorting are fairly high with sorting capability up to 32 fields. Each field can be sorted in either ascending or descending sequence. If that is not enough, you can even adjust the collating sequence to force different sort patters.

Collating Sequence

Every now and then, there is some piece of data or a data element that you may prefer to take a different sequence in your output report. For example, if you had a need to make the letter "b" have the collating value of an "a,." The Query/400 product enables you to do this. You just define an entry in a collating table that gives the "b" a priority over the letter "a." By implementing such a change, the b's would come before all the *a's* in your report.

Column Formatting

The product provides extensive report formatting options, column and row formatting, prompt editing, spacing adjustments, etc. When the report is very wide, by changing the spacing and print width of fields, reports can be structured so that all record data fits on one line.

With the column formatting options, you can control how output from your query is to look in your report. For example, you can change the spacing before the report columns, the headings above the columns, and the report field lengths. You can also change the editing characteristics for a numeric field. You can either specify numeric field editing values or you can supply edit words to customize the look and feel of any field which is in your report.

Report Summaries

Quite often you may need to produce a report, in which totals, averages and/or other summary information are needed. The Select Report Summary Functions display allows you to specify for any and all fields that are included in your query report. You can get totals, averages, minimum values, maximum values, and counts. All functions can be used for numeric fields, and all except total and average can be used for character, date, time, and timestamp fields. Your report can include all the detail and the final totals, or just the final totals.

Report Breaks

Sometimes final summaries are not enough, and a detail report would be too much. The Define Report Breaks facility can be used to increase your options so that you can get either detailed reports with periodic summations or you can just get a report of summations with final totals. You use this facility to define all the report-breaks that you want to occur in your Query report. These are used to arrange the report into sections, each time the value of a break-field, changes.

When a report break occurs for a group of records, such as all the records for a particular customer, summary information for just that customer appears in the Query report.

On each summary function line caused by a report break,, the Query/400 program provides the name of the function, such as "Customer average." Additionally, the Query provides all of the summary values that are calculated for that report break.

Output Type and Form

Query/400 also offers a number of report level options. For example, the menu option for selecting the output type and output form lets you select where you want your Query output to go, and in what form you want it to be. In other words, you can have the output displayed, printed, or put into a database file. You can also specify that the output is to be in detailed form or in summary form.

When you choose not to specify, Query uses many defaults. Most of these are pretty good. If you do not define the output type when defining your Query, for example, the output produced by the query is a displayed report in detailed form.

This option also provides you the ability to add a report title and page headings and footers to the output report. Additionally there are options to control the printout or name the database depending on the type of Query output you define.

Processing Options

The last set of options that are provided by Query, are subtle and are typically not specified when you build a Query. In fact, some options would only be understood by programmers. Most users take the defaults to these. The *Specify Processing Options* display lets you specify the processing options to be used when the query is run. For example, you can specify the following:

1.   Whether the results should be rounded.

2.   Whether bad decimal data is ignored.

3.   Whether character substitution is ignored, or treated as an error when character conversion occurs. This can occur, for example, if you are joining with two fields that have different CCSIDs (internal codes.)

4.   Whether the collating sequence (discussed above) is used for all character comparisons.

Summary

The Query process involves selecting files, fields, and records, and sorting those records into a desired sequence. Additionally, you may add report, column, and page headings and footers. You can also use column headings from the database as your report default, or you can create your own headings. You can also pick fields for minor, intermediate, and various levels of major totals. Additionally, you can opt for final totals, averages, as well as counts, and minimum or maximum value functions. You can then send your query to a database, a display, or a printer.

When it is necessary to create new fields for your report, Query/400 provides a powerful results-field facility. The record selection process involves creating up to 100 comparison tests that Query uses to select the desired records. The tests can be made against database fields or the result fields. If the result of the test or the combined result of several tests is true, the record being tested is selected and included in your query output. The types of tests used are: equal, not equal, less than or equal, greater than, less than, greater than or equal, range, list (contents of the field is equal to one of the values in a list), and like (contents of the field has a pattern similar to the value).

Editing of numeric fields can be taken from database file, or you can specify editing during Query definition. You can sort up to 32 different fields in either ascending, or descending sequence. The report formatting options include page heading and footing, column heading, report breaks at subtotals, totals, averages, minimum or maximum values, and ejects for each page. Of course, you have the option of sorting the report in ascending or descending sequence, using up to six different data fields.

Query for Everybody

When IBM was in its heyday, selling AS/400 systems from its Branch Offices, in addition to the Application Development Tool Set (ADTS) and the RPG compiler, the Query product became a staple in every new AS/400 client's arsenal. Since, ultimately, IBM held its field reps and systems engineers accountable for customer satisfaction, and no package ever supplied all of the reports a company ever needed, IBM's local sales force made sure that there was enough money in the budget for the Query product.

Even today, IBM's business partners continue the tradition of selling Query/400 to every customer. This is not the case for all products, such as SQL, which is still not on the *everybody-gets* list. Even though, just as SQL, ADTS, and RPG, a Query/400 customer must pay for the product separately, nobody would want to take the risk of not offering the Query/400 product to fill in the data gaps as required.

No OfficeVision Links

If IBM consistently put resources back into the products from which they gain revenue, Query/400 research would be well funded. Though, in most cases, IBM seems to invest where the revenue stream exists, Query is a big exception. Still a big seller, and purchased separately with each new AS/400 and iSeries, Query has not been enhanced substantially for years. Even its documentation is out-of-date. Of course, that makes this book even more worthwhile.

In doing some final research for the conversion of the original stand-up education QuikCourse to this text based tutorial, I thought it would be a good idea to check out the current Query/400 manual. I did. It's not! Current, that is! I found references about coming from DisplayWrite 4, which has long been eclipsed in favor of other non-

IBM PC word processors, and I also saw a number of references to the text/merge facilities with OfficeVision/400 which IBM canned at Version 5, Release1.

I guess since the IBM developers know that they have not enhanced Query in a long time so, they have not bothered to tell the writers of the reference manuals to bring the product's documentation up-to-date with the product interfaces for those products which no longer are supported by IBM.

The good news, about IBM's product documentation, is that it is actually very good. You will find it worth the trip to the Web. There, you can get free documentation to help support your Query activities. To help you find the Query documentation and other IBM manuals on the Web, we have included a road map to IBM manuals in Appendix A. of this book.

Form Follows Function

It's actually too bad for all of us that IBM has not invested substantially in Query/400. If the product made incremental steps, and if it were given a Web interface, it could very well be as good as it gets. The fact is that Query/400 in its green screen state is not bad at all. Unfortunately, IBM had other plans. However, I still don't know what those other plans are since Query/400 is still the hot IBM seller and it is still the most used Report Writer on the AS/400 and iSeries. I just have to visit my account set to know that.

Having said that, Query/400 does offer very nice functions. IBM should update its form. Since form should follow function, with Query/400 IBM has a winner and a market winner to boot.

Chapter 2   Getting Query Started / Query Management

Typical Start

Like most interactive (green screen) IBM products, new users can start Query with its start command, *STRQRY*. After you get a few Queries under your belt, however, you will more than likely move to the *Work With Queries* command - *WRKQRY*, which has less work for the same utility. For queries already defined and built by, or for others, you will use *RUNQRY*. Overall, you will find STRQRY a bit too much work.

When queries become stale, rather than STRQRY to delete them with a menu, you will choose another command - *DLTQRY*. This is the *Delete Query* command. Just as IBM's Data File Utility (DFU) with which you may be familiar, after you create your definition, you get to save it as a "program." Once the Query definition is saved, you can then work with it, run it, or delete it. You do not need to go through an ad-hoc query build for each repetitive query. Just save it once and run it each time you need it. And, when the query is no longer needed, just as with DFU, you can delete its definition.

Fire it Up!

Let's start Query/400 now with the most logical command for beginners - *STRQRY*. When you issue a *STRQRY*, you are presented with a menu such as that in Figure 1-1,

Figure 1-1 STRQRY Menu

```
QUERY                        Query Utilities
                                           System:    HELLO
Select one of the following:

  Query for AS/400
    1. Work with queries
    2. Run an existing query
    3. Delete a query

  DB2 for AS/400
   10. Start DB2 Query Manager for AS/400

  Query management
   20. Work with query management forms
   21. Work with query management queries
   22. Start a query
   23. Analyze a Query for AS/400 definition
                                                    More...

   24. Start a query allowing Query for AS/400 definitions

  Related menus
   30. Files
   31. Office tasks

Selection or command
===>

F3=Exit   F4=Prompt   F9=Retrieve   F12=Cancel   F13=Info Assistant
F16=AS/400 Main menu
```

The First Several Options

Notice that the first three options are *WRKQRY*, *RUNQRY*, and *DLTQRY*, respectively. Since we will not be working with the options following # 3 very much in this QuikCourse, we will give a brief explanation of these options before we proceed with the rest of the QuikCourse. You will find that most of the later options have to do with something called AS/400 Query Management (QM).

Query Management

So, before we cover these options, just what is Query Management? Among other things it is the following:

1. A standard system programming interface into database and query access

2. A collection of commands that can be coded into a program to run a query and generate a report

3. Designed for use by programmers and technical people

4. Integrated into the OS/400 Operating System

Not an End User Interface

It will also help you to know that Query Management is not an end-user interface which can help you define or change queries and report formatting. You won't be using it at all in this book. Yet, for you to have a complete look at what is provided with Query, we described each of the Query Management options below at a general level. Though they are prominently highlighted, I do not believe they should be on the main Query product menu.

Of course, I don't think delete and run should be on the menu either. The STRQRY should bring us to a menu in a fashion similar to DFU and PDM (Program Development Manager - the main list tool for developers). These provide the pertinent options for the task at hand.

The QM options have nothing to do with the Query/400 product. IBM also ships a programmer interface to Query known as OPNQRYF (Open Query File). This is a low level command for programmers to do queries within CL programs. It has nothing to do with Query/400, and therefore it is not on the menu. The QM options again should not be on the STRQRY menu.

In fact, they make the product appear cumbersome, as opposed to easy and inviting. Their existence forces a user to wonder what they are all about. All the while, they serve little useful purpose for the Query/400 function.

Having said that, I suspect you will want to see for yourself, so, here are the options, along with their option numbers from the menu.

10. Start DB2 Query Manager for AS/400

Select this option to start Query Manager. This option allows you to build, manage, and run SQL queries, create reports, and use the table editing feature of Query Manager. If you have SQL installed, you may get some benefit from QM.

It would help to know that there are two external query creation interfaces with AS/400 and iSeries. The first is the AS/400 Query product, which we are learning, and the second is the Query Manager for AS/400. This one depends upon the SQL product being installed on your AS/400 or iSeries.

Since the Query Manager product (SQL) is a charge product, which many AS/400 shops **do not** have, and SQL does not supply a menu option for Query/400, which is a also charge product , I do not think it is necessary, or appropriate, for Query/400 users to have the QM Options on the STRQRY menu.

If you happen to take this option (Option 10), after you thought you had just started AS/400 Query with the STRQRY command, you are now going to exit Query/400 and run QM. If you really want to use Query Manager, the command STRQM works fine without the stop off on the AS/400 Query menu. Ironically, there are no Query/400 options on the STRQM menu.

20. Work with Query Management Forms

The *Work With Query Management Forms* (*WRKQMFORM*) command is executed from this menu option. This command is the first part of a system interface to building Queries. It is ugly. To use this, you do not need either the AS/400 Query product, or the IBM Query Manager, which come with the SQL product. You just need a lot of time, since it is not easy to use. The good news is that you don't need it. Do not take this option.

21. Work with Query Management Queries

The *Work With Query Management Queries (WRKQMQRY)* command is executed from this menu option. This command is the second and final part of a system interface to building queries without having either the AS/400 Query product, or the IBM Query Manager modules which come with the SQL product. Again, you don't need it.

22. Start a Query

This option executes the *Start Query Management Query (STRQMQRY)* command, which is used to run a QM query. The query is any single Structured Query Language (SQL) statement in a QMQRY object. It has nothing to do with Query/400, the object of our study. However, for programmers, it may help to know that the SQL statement can also be taken from a *query definition (QRYDFN)* object, built by Query/400, when a QMQRY object does not exist. Again, you really do not need this option if you have Query/400.

23. Analyze a Query for AS/400 Definition

This option invokes the *Analyze Query (ANZQRY)* command, and allows you to analyze a query definition object (QRYDFN). Though QRYDFN objects are from Query/400, the purpose of this command is to see if your QUERY/400 queries can be converted to QM. Thus, this command checks your query for potential Query Management conversion problems.

If it will not convert, you will get diagnostic messages about potential differences between Query/400 and Query Management use of query and form information, which is derived from the analyzed QRYDFN object.

This command has value only for those who want to run their AS/400 queries within a system query framework, or for those moving to IBM's Query Manager, and who want to take their queries with them. If you are just learning Query/400, you do not need this option.

These are all the options you get on panel 1 of the STRQRY menu. However, the menu is more than one panel. I scrolled down the menu and pasted the three remaining options into Figure 1-1, so that we could discuss the menu logically as one item. Here are the rest of the options.

24. Start a Query Allowing Query for AS/400 Definitions

This option is similar to option 22, except you can specify an AS/400 Query definition, and the Query Management process will try to execute your AS/400 query. Again, this is not needed.

30. Files

Option 30 is handy in that it gives you a host of file commands to use. It does nothing, however to help you build a query. Unless it has value for you in this context, you do not need it. I do not use it.

31. Office Tasks

When OfficeVision/400 (OV/400) was viable, this provided valuable linkage to the document facilities within OV/400. I view this option on the Query menu as vestigial. It is like the appendix in the human body. You once might have needed it, but IBM took away the OV/400 function which it provided at one time, so you don't need it any more.

STRQRY Options

After that trip down mostly useless options, let's go back to those that
can help us in the Query/400 game. If you select option 2 (Run an
Existing Query), and press enter, the prompt displays for the
RUNQRY command. Use this to select an existing query to produce
your desired query report.

If you select option 3 (Delete a Query), and press enter, you are
shown the prompt displays for the DLTQRY command. You can
use this to delete a query definition. These options are further
explained in Chapters 17 and 18. Now, let's see what is cooking in
Chapter 3.

Chapter 3   Work With Queries

File Definition

The best way to demonstrate the utility of a program like Query/400
is to use it for a practical purpose. In another Kelly Consulting
QuikCourse, AS/400 Database, we introduced a file called the
VENDORP. It is a physical database file that was built with a
"dictionary" file as a reference. It is a simple file with just ten fields.
You will use this file as the basis for a Query case study, which we
call the VENDORP case study. The database description for the
VENDORP file is shown in Figure 3-2.

The VENDORP Case Study

The Data Description Specifications (DDS) in Figure 3-2 represent
the database coding necessary to create the VENDORP file. We will
not be using the file in this chapter, but now the information is
available to us. You now know it exits. Unless you are a
programmer, however, you are more than likely not too familiar with
DDS. That's OK. You don't have to be good at DDS to usc Qucry.
DDS is what programmers use to define databases.

When you are defining your queries, the query product will present
the data elements of VENDORP to you in a more meaningful
fashion than DDS. Don't worry, you do not have to remember this
DDS to understand the Query examples.

Near the end of this QuikCourse (Chapter 19), you will see that we
add another file to the mix. Once we have the two related files, you
will learn how to produce a JOIN Query. In this way, you will taste
the full range of query capabilities by the time you finish this

QuikCourse. The second file (an item file) is defined in the JOIN case study later in the book.

Help! QuickCourse F in the original classroom courses has also been converted to text form. It is now a book. The iSeries Database Pocket Developers Guide is now available from LETS GO PUBLISH and many popular AS/400 and iSeries Book Publishers and Distributors.

Figure 3-2 VENDORP File

```
Columns . . . :   1  71                  Edit
HELLO/QDDSSRC
  SEU==> _____        VENDORP

        *************** Beginning of data ***************************
 0001.00       A*   VENDOR MASTER PHYSICAL FILE
 0002.00       A                          REF(FIELDREF)
 0003.00       A           R VNDMSTR      TEXT('VENDMAST DB FORMAT')
 0004.00       A             VNDNBR    R
 0005.00       A             NAME      R
 0006.00       A             ADDR1     R
 0007.00       A             CITY      R
 0008.00       A             STATE     R
 0009.00       A             ZIPCD     R
 0010.00       A             VNDCLS    R
 0011.00       A             VNDSTS    R
 0012.00       A             BALOWE    R
 0013.00       A             SRVRTG    R
        ***************** End of data ***************************
 F3=Exit   F4=Prompt    F5=Rfsh   F9=Retrieve   F10=Cursor   F11=Toggle
 F16=Repeat find        F17=Repeat change          F24=More keys
```

Work With Queries Panel

To get re-started, let's select the Work with Queries option, by taking option 1 from the STRQRY menu, which is shown in Figure 3-3 for your convenience.

Figure 3-3 Normal STRQRY Menu

```
QUERY                        Query Utilities
                                           System:    HELLO
Select one of the following:
  Query for AS/400
    1. Work with queries
    2. Run an existing query
    3. Delete a query

  DB2 for AS/400
    10. Start DB2 Query Manager for AS/400

  Query management
    20. Work with query management forms
    21. Work with query management queries
    22. Start a query
    23. Analyze a Query for AS/400 definition
                                              More...

Selection or command
===> 1

F3=Exit    F4=Prompt    F9=Retrieve    F12=Cancel    F13=Info Assistant
F16=AS/400 Main menu
```

When you select option 1, press ENTER.

As a point of note, if you were not using the STRQRY menu, you could type the command WRKQRY on an interactive command line and press ENTER. Either way, the Work With Queries display is shown as in Figure 3-4.

Figure 3-4 Work With Queries

```
                         Work with Queries

Type choices, press Enter.

    Option  . . . . .   1          1=Create,2=Chnge, 3=Copy, 4=Delete
                                   5=Display, 6=Print definition
                                   8=Run in batch, 9=Run
    Query . . . . . . FIRSTQ ____  Name, F4 for list
       Library . . . . HELLO ____  Name, *LIBL, F4 for list


  F3=Exit      F4=Prompt     F5=Refresh      F12=Cancel
                                   (C) COPYRIGHT IBM CORP. 1988
```

Creating a New Query

In the Work With Queries panel, as shown in Figure 3-4, you specify which query you want to work with (FIRSTQ) and in what way (Create). From this menu, you can do a lot more than create a query, however. You can see all your options to the right of the option prompt. In addition to creating a query, you can also change, copy, delete, display, print, or run a query in batch or interactive mode.

You can see in Figure 3-4, that we are staged to create a query. Option 1 is already filled in. Below the option, you can type the name you are going to give to your new query (FIRSTQ). If you type the name, you also type the library (HELLO) in which you want to store the completed query definition.

To Name or Not To Name?

You really do not have to name your query, unless you want to save it for later use. In Figure 3-4, you see that we did name the query, but you can just as easily type option 1, and press ENTER without supplying a name. Whether you name your query or not, when you hit the ENTER key, you will be taken to the Define the Query panel as shown in Figure 3-5.

Figure 3-5 Define The Query Panel

```
                         Define the Query
  Query . . . . . . :    FIRSTQ        Option . . . . . :    CREATE
  Library . . . . :     HELLO          CCSID . . . . . . :    37
  Type options, press Enter.  Press F21 to select all.
     1=Select

  Opt     Query Definition Option
          Specify file selections
          Define result fields
          Select and sequence fields
          Select records
          Select sort fields
          Select collating sequence
          Specify report column formatting
          Select report summary functions
          Define report breaks
          Select output type and output form
          Specify processing options


   F3=Exit          F5=Report        F12=Cancel              F13=Layout
   F18=Files        F21=Select all
```

Of course, if you did not name your query, the name FIRSTQ would not be shown at the top of this panel.

Existing Queries

Before we move on to Chapter 4, where we cover the panel shown in Figure 3-5, let's briefly talk about how you go about working with queries which already exist. Please note that the WRKQRY menu is covered in detail in Chapter 17. In Chapter 5, we come back to creating the VENDORP case study query, after this diversion. Since most shops already have queries built, this section has value in that it will quickly help you learn how to find them.

Why Query At All?

First of all, why do you want to do a query? You typically would invoke the Query program when you want information from the database that is not available through the options provided by your software package and/or your personal menus. In other words, you use Query when you have a need for information.

Many Queries But Where?

The natural thing to do when you need answers is to go to Query/400 and try to create a definition which gives you what you need. However, this may not serve you well if this is a regular routine. It is very likely that, unless your system is new, somebody has already built many of the queries that will provide you with the information you need. Your problem, of course is to find them.

The Name Matters

Even if you are the first person to use Query/400 in the shop, which is very unlikely, you probably don't want to create a new query definition for each of your requests. Therefore, it would be prudent to name your queries, document them, and organize them in a way that helps you know what they are and what they do. In this way, you will at least be able to find your own queries.

IT Knows How To Find Them?

If your organization is not new to Query, however, then you should ask your IT folks how to make sense of the stored queries. Hopefully, your IT shop has used some logic in helping the users organize their queries so that each new query is not a new and unique project. This can save lots of time. The quickest way to get something done in IT is to find out, just before you build it, that it is already done. So also with queries.

Use Query to Find Queries

Query/400 provides some tools to help you find queries, though the methods are not very sophisticated. For example, if you think that there may already be a query to satisfy the needs of a request, you can take a look at all the queries in a particular library. You would scan each query to see if one is suitable as is, or with some minor modifications. Of course, this can be very time consuming. Before we show some better methods, you may be wondering how to do the scan. We'll show you now.

The WRKQRY command, which we first showed in Figure 1-4, has a few tricks which can help in finding queries. We repeat this panel below as Figure 3-6 for your convenience.

Figure 3-6 Work With Queries

```
                          Work with Queries

  Type choices, press Enter.

      Option  . . . . . .   2           1=Create, 2=Change, 3=Copy, 4=Delete
                                        5=Display, 6=Print definition
                                        8=Run in batch, 9=Run
      Query . . . . . . .               Name, F4 for list
         Library . . . . .    HELLO     Name, *LIBL, F4 for list




  F3=Exit      F4=Prompt      F5=Refresh      F12=Cancel
                                             (C) COPYRIGHT IBM CORP. 1988
```

Before we return to Create a Query from this panel, let us explore
how we would find already-built queries. Instead of taking option 1
on the Work With Queries menus, as shown in Figure 3-4, take
option 2. For the library, type the library name in which you would
like to store your queries.

We used the HELLO library in the example shown in Figure 3-6. For
the query name, do not supply any value. That is the trick. Instead,
position the cursor on the blank line, and press F4. You will then see
a panel very similar to that in Figure 3-7.

Figure 3-7 Work With Queries

```
                 Work with Queries


Library . . . . . . . .  HELLO    Name, *LIBL, F4 for list

Subset  . . . . . . . .  ___     Name, generic*

Position to . . . . . .  ___     Starting characters


Type options (and Query), press Enter.

 1=Create  2=Change  3=Copy  4=Delete  5=Display  6=Print

 8=Run in batch  9=Run

Opt  Query      Text                     Changed

 2

 _  ACCTTRPAYP   print payment history and current      03/12/02

 _  ACCTTRPAY1   Payments from HSTRCPTS to file         03/12/02

 _  ACCTTRPAY2   List Payments cashrcpts to a file      03/12/02

 _  ADJUSTCIGS   Print Daily inventory Adjustments      06/27/02

 _  ADJUSTFCUM   Print Daily inventory Adjustments      03/20/01

 _  ADJUSTMENT   Print Daily inventory Adjustments      04/15/02

 _  ADPAGES     1/2 + Full Page Sales Sum(CHG DEFINE RESULT)  06/05/01

 _  AIRHEAD      AIRHEAD VELOCITY REPORT 2ND QUARTER PROMOTIO  07/17/00

 _  AIRHEADFB    Select Airheads for Promo Report       07/17/00

                        More...

F3=Exit    F4=Prompt    F5=Refresh   F11=Display names only

F12=Cancel   F19=Next group
```

Rolling, Rolling, Rolling

You can see in the Hello Library in Figure 3-7 above, that there are nine queries listed. Notice the "More" sign in the bottom right corner. That means there are more queries. To find them, you can use the Page Up and Page Down keys (a.k.a. roll keys) to move through the list of queries. The more queries you have, obviously, the more rolls you have to do to find the desired query. Yes, it can be a lot of work finding a query.

Help From IBM

IBM has provided a tool to help you get through all these queries, without getting a sore Roll finger. If you want to see a smaller group of query names, just type the starting characters next to the Subset prompt at the top of the Work with Queries panel (Figure 3-7). Follow the text with an "*," to identify the group you want to see; then press ENTER.

Subset Caveat

If you do not use the "*," only the one query with a name that exactly matches your specific subset name is shown. With the "*," all the queries whose names begin with those characters preceding the "*," from the specified library or library list, are shown. When you want to return to the full list of query names, just blank out the subset prompt, or put an "*" in it, and again press ENTER.

Position To

There is one more tool which can also help you work with existing queries. If you want to see more than a subset, such as all the queries that start with FC and all those that follow FC, you can use the Position to prompt, which is right under subset at the top of the Work with Queries panel. To position the list of query names, so that it starts with a particular name or sequence of characters, type all of the characters, or one or more of the starting characters of the name you want, and press ENTER

Unlike subset, you do not have to add an "*" after the starting characters in this prompt. If there is no query name in the list that starts with those characters, Query positions the list to the name closest to, and in front of, the position where the name would have appeared. When you are ready to return to the full list, at the top of the queries, type "*TOP". To go to the end of the list of queries, type "*BOT". Use the Page or Roll keys to move forward or backward through the list of queries as you would normally.

In summary, the IBM tools are not the greatest to help you find a long lost query, but they help. Use Subset when you are reasonably confident that you have a name clue, since no names after the subset will be shown. With Position To, you get a nice starting point from which you can roll through to the end of the names.

Text Field Is Important

The Text field is next to the query name. This provides you a means of describing your query, and it also helps in finding queries. Though Query is a big revenue winner in IBM, IBM development has never built a search engine to help you find your queries. It would be nice if they did. There is still time, IBM.

Though I would recommend you always use the text field to further document your queries, there is no means to search this field for possible query definition hits, when you are looking for a pre-built query. The text is necessary, so that when you locate a query candidate, you can know that the query suits your needs, without you having to open it up.

Changed Field Helps

The Changed field also helps in locating and differentiating queries. If you know your query is just about six months old, as you are scanning, you can reject all the entries that are older or newer than the query for which you are searching.

Find Queries Summary

In summary, then, to find existing queries, from the panel in Figure 3-6, you can fill in the library name, and position the cursor on the Query Name prompt, and press F4. This shows a list of all the queries that are in the library specified. Of course, the FIRSTQ query name, which you are in the process of creating, would not be in the list since you are just now about to create it. But, you might find something worth using, and FIRSTQ might not be necessary.

For education purposes at this point, fill in the necessary fields, as shown in Figure 3-6, and press ENTER. You will then see the main Query panel in Figure 3-8. You can't get to Figure 3-8 without having seen the panel in Figure 3-6.

Chapter 4   Define the Query Panel

The Major Panel

The Define the Query panel, in Figure 3-8, is a major staple for this QuikCourse. There are a few unique attributes of the panel, which we will discuss now, so that you can remember them later. You may recall from Chapter 3 that you can get to this panel by taking option 1 (CREATE) on the Work With Queries panel.

Please note that you will see this panel at least ten more times before we finish all of the chapters in this QuikCourse.

Figure 4-1 Define The Query Panel

```
                         Define the Query
  Query . . . . . . :   FIRSTQ          Option . . . . . :   CREATE
  Library . . . . :    HELLO           CCSID . . . . . . :     37
  Type options, press Enter.  Press F21 to select all.
    1=Select

  Opt    Query Definition Option
   1     Specify file selections
         Define result fields
         Select and sequence fields
         Select records
         Select sort fields
         Select collating sequence
         Specify report column formatting
         Select report summary functions
         Define report breaks
         Select output type and output form
         Specify processing options

   F3=Exit          F5=Report         F12=Cancel
   F13=Layout       F18=Files         F21=Select all
```

Un-numbered Menu Options

First of all, as you can see, there are 11 un-numbered options in the panel. That is a healthy list of options. Unfortunately, because there is no tag, such as a number or letter, the menu options will be a little bit more difficult to discuss.

> Note: As we go through each of the 11 definition options in detail, we continually refer to the Define the Query panel. To make it easier to follow along, we repeat this panel for each option, before working the option. Then, we show the incremental change indicating completion after working the option. Additionally, the option being discussed is highlighted and is shown in the menu title.

Full Coverage

So that it is easier for you to know which option we are covering, we will move down the list in the Define the Query panel (shown in Figure I-8 and other places in this book), one option at a time. We will also refer to the option by name as we present it. Also worthy of note, is that there is only one selection designator ("1") to use with the options on the panel.

Use "1" as Your Checkmark

Place a "1" as a selection designator in much the same way as you would use an "X" or a check-mark. It is easy to assume that the "1" filled next to Specify file selections in Figure I-8, pertains to file selections just because file selections is the first menu option. When you get to the second option, Define result fields, the selection designator continues to be a "1." It does not become a "2" for the second option. Just as with Specify file selections, when you want to work with result fields, you place a "1" next to the option and press ENTER.

The Right Sequence

One of the beauties of the Define the Query panel as shown in Figure I-8, is that it is organized almost perfectly. If you go down the panel one option at a time, selecting the options you need to satisfy your query, it is hard to go wrong. Like everything else in life, with practice, your eyes will open wider on each of these options. Over time, they will all have more meaning.

In just a short while, in Chapter 5, you will resume a Query exercise. The first part of every Query and thus every Query exercise is to select the file(s) for the Query. From this point, you will begin to learn Query/400 by taking all the menu options in sequence to solve the VENDORP case study.. Before we make the jump to the practical, let's quickly check out each of these menu options for defining Queries.

The Define the Query Options

The first set of options are for selecting files, result fields, database fields, records, sort fields, and for changing the collating sequence. The second set of options are for report writing and special formatting for report breaks and totals. The second to last option is for selecting your output type and form - display, printer or database, and whether the report should be detailed or summary. The last Option allows for numeric results information to be specified, such as data decimal checking and rounding.

How To Select

On the Define the Query panel, you type a 1 next to the options you need. You can type them one at a time or type all the 1's you need at the beginning. You can also press F21 to select all of the query options. From this display you can select the options that define the four major parts of the query definition.

And the Option Groupings Are?

The first six options define the Query itself, including what files you want to query, what fields are to be used in each file and what records are to be selected. The next three options define what the report is to look like, including which columns are to be summarized, and where the report breaks are going to be.

The second to the last option defines where the report is to be sent (printer, disk, display) and what values are to be used when it is sent there.

The last option defines how numeric results are processed and how characters are formed and used.

Not All Options Are Used

Not many Query users select all the options when creating a Query. Just as a menu at a fine diner, you need select only the options that you desire. There is no requirement to review the defaults. If you do not pick an option, you get whatever the defaults are. You may find, as many Query users do, that the defaults for many options are quite acceptable. Not having to specify them permits you to define your Query much faster.

Keeping Track of Your Progress

One more thing! When you are working through the Define the Query menu, you will notice that Query/400 keeps track of the options that you have used. It places a greater than sign ">" next to each option as you work with it. When you finish your Query, you will have these ">" signs speckled to the left of the menu options. This assists you in knowing what you have done while building the Query and it also helps later when you call up an existing Query definition for modification.

Well, there you have it. The Define Query Menu is the most important menu in the Query/400 product. It is your springboard to success for using Query/400 on your AS/400 or iSeries. Now, let' start taking some options from this very important menu.

Chapter 5   Picking the File to Query

File Selections

Now that we have a 20,000 foot perspective on the Define The Query menu, let's revert to where we were in Chapter 3, when we false started our first Create Query. As you may recall, we began to create the FIRSTQ query.

As a point of note, it will help to remember that when you create your Query/400 definition, and perhaps later, you change his query or another query on your system, you'll find that the steps for both creating, and changing a query are quite similar.

The major difference is that when you change a query, you need to pick only those menu options that you want to change. This may be all of the options you selected on the Create, a subset of the menu options used on the Create, or it can be a combination of options used on the Create, and new options, which you are providing. As new options are added, Query/400 places the tell-tale ">" sign in front of the option, to help you more easily manage the query.

Notice that in Figure 5-1, the Define the Query panel has no items with the selected indicator ">" displayed.

Figure 5-1 Define The Query Panel

```
                              Define the Query
Query . . . . . . :     FIRSTQ       Option . . . . . :     CREATE
Library . . . . :       HELLO        CCSID . . . . . . :     37
Type options, press Enter.  Press F21 to select all.
  1=Select


Opt     Query Definition Option
 1      Specify file selections
        Define result fields
        Select and sequence fields
        Select records
        Select sort fields
        Select collating sequence
        Specify report column formatting
        Select report summary functions
        Define report breaks
        Select output type and output form
        Specify processing options


 F3=Exit           F5=Report          F12=Cancel
 F13=Layout        F18=Files          F21=Select all
```

Select Your File(s)

Let's move on to selecting the file or files for your query. In Chapter 3, you saw the DDS for the VENDORP file. This is the file we will now use for this query. You select the file for your Query by typing a "1" next to the Specify file selections option, as shown in Figure 5-1. Then, press the ENTER key. For your efforts, the panel in Figure 5-2 appears.

Well, not exactly! When you first tell Query/400 that you are going to create a query, it knows that you cannot create a query, without having a database file defined in the query. So, the first time, Query/400 shows you the Define the Query panel, it automatically plugs in the "1" to Select the Files option. You don't have to do it because it is done for you.

After you fill in the file information and you move on, Query/400 removes the "1" and puts a greater than ">" sign next to the option. Before you end your query definition session, you can always go back, and reselect Specify File Selections to change or add file information.

Figure 5-2 Pick Your Files

```
                        Specify File Selections

 Type choices, press Enter.  Press F9 to specify an additional
    file selection.

    File . . . . . . . . . .            Name, F4 for list
       Library  . . . . . .    *LIBL    Name, *LIBL, F4 for list
    Member . . . . . . . .    *FIRST___  Name, *FIRST, F4 for list
    Format . . . . . . . .    *FIRST___  Name, *FIRST, F4 for list


  F3=Exit         F4=Prompt      F5=Report            F9=Add file
  F12=Cancel      F13=Layout     F18=Files
```

Type It In

In the panel shown in Figure 5-2, you identify the file, library, member name, and format name that you wish to query. The system can help you identify any of these four prompted items, if you would like some help. Just press F4 on the option line for option-specific help.

The first help you naturally get is that the system default for the library prompt is to use the library list. Next to the Library prompt you can see the term *LIBL. This is the AS/400's abbreviation for the User's Library List.

Library List

Every signed-on user is given a list of libraries referenced from the user profile. If you do not know what library your file is in, but you believe it is in one of the libraries which would be in your list of libraries, then it is perfectly OK to permit this prompt to continue with *LIBL, as defaulted in Figure 5-2.

Members

You get help, again, in that the default for Member is *FIRST. You probably have already noticed that the AS/400 and iSeries likes to use the "*" as a starting character for its default terms. The term *FIRST refers to the first member in the file that you select for the query.

Files can have up to 32,767 members. A member is like a subdivision of a file. An invoice file, for example, might have a member for each day of the week. However, most files have only one member. Moreover, most files are not subdivided. Therefore, by taking this bit of help from Query/400, defaulting to the first member of a file, you will almost always be right. In almost all cases, you will get the first and only member of the file. Unless told otherwise by your IT staff, always use *FIRST for the member prompt.

Formats

There can be up to 32 different formats in a logical file. A format is like a record layout. A physical file can have just one format and most logical files have just one format. Therefore, when defining queries, *FIRST is always appropriate for physical files, and almost always appropriate for logical files. For physical files, there is no thinking required. For logicals, it is a safe bet to leave it at first, until proven wrong. If proven wrong, try to get some help from your IT staff.

Formal Cursor-Sensitive Help Lists

There is another way to get some help, rather than take the Query/400 defaults. For example, if you position the cursor to any of the four prompt lines in Figure 5-2, and you press F4, you will get a panel with any of the following lists, depending on where your cursor was positioned:

1.   List of file names in the library list
2.   List of libraries in the library list
3.   List of members in the library
4.   List of formats in the member

This comes in really handy when you are looking for a specific file, and you are not prepared to take the defaults. From the lists that are given, you can select the values appropriate for your query.

In most cases, after you begin your query adventures, you will know the file name and the library name of the file you want to query. You probably will not have much need for the list capability, but knowing it is there may help you in the future. You will more than likely specify the file and the library, as shown on Figure 5-3.

Figure 5-3 Pick Your Files

```
                        Specify File Selections

  Type choices, press Enter.  Press F9 to specify an additional
     file selection.

     File . . . . . . . . . .   VENDORP      Name, F4 for list
        Library  . . . . . . .    HELLO       Name, *LIBL, F4 for list
     Member . . . . . . . . .   *FIRST___    Name, *FIRST, F4 for list
     Format . . . . . . . . .   *FIRST___    Name, *FIRST, F4 for list




  F3=Exit          F4=Prompt        F5=Report           F9=Add file
  F12=Cancel       F13=Layout       F18=Files
```

You can specify as many as 32 files to be queried, and you can assign unique, 3 character identifiers to each one, to help in field differentiation in other areas of the query definition. We demonstrate this in the JOIN case study near the end of this QuikCourse.

Completing the Files Panel

In Figure 5-3, you get to pick the first file you want to query and the library in which it resides. The defaults for the member are to take the first member and the first format. When you press ENTER after the file selection, the format names will drop into the Format prompt slot and let you choose to confirm it, or not.

More Than One File

In this VENDORP query case study, just type in VENDORP as the name of the query and HELLO as the library. If, in another query, you must specify more than one file, for a JOIN multi-file query, you would press F9. By pressing F9, the panel opens up, requesting your information required for the second and subsequent files. A panel similar to that in Figure 5-4 would appear.

Figure 5-4 Pick Your Files -More Than One

```
                         Specify File Selections

Type choices, press Enter.  Press F9 to specify an additional
   file selection.

   File . . . . . . . . .   VENDORP      Name, F4 for list
      Library  . . . . . .    HELLO      Name, *LIBL, F4 for list
   Member . . . . . . . .   *FIRST       Name, *FIRST, F4 for list
   Format . . . . . . . .   *FIRST       Name, *FIRST, F4 for list
   File ID  . . . . . . .   T01          A Z99, *ID

   File . . . . . . . . .                Name, F4 for list
      Library  . . . . . .    HELLO      Name, *LIBL, F4 for list
   Member . . . . . . . .   *FIRST       Name, *FIRST, F4 for list
   Format . . . . . . . .   *FIRST       Name, *FIRST, F4 for list
   File ID  . . . . . . .   *ID          A Z99, *ID

Bottom
F3=Exit           F4=Prompt          F5=Report           F9=Add file
F12=Cancel        F13=Layout         F24=More Keys
```

File IDs Are Used in JOIN

In the JOIN case study in Chapter 19, we will demonstrate how to fill
out the information for the second file. Other than the file ID, which
we are about to explain, it is all the same as for the first file.

If you compare the panel in Figure 5-2 with that of Figure 5-4, you
notice that there is no file ID field for the same file when it is
specified alone. This prompt is not shown if only one file selection
group has been used, and you have not yet pressed F9 for additional
file selection prompts.

File IDs are 3 character identifiers, that are used in combination with
identical field names in a JOIN query, so that you know which file a
particular field is associated with.

The file IDs are used on other query definition displays, as you will
see in the JOIN case study. They are placed in front of, and as part
of, all the field names used in your query definition whenever they
are displayed in lists. You will type file IDs on some displays as part
of a field name whenever there is a possibility that the same field
name is used in more than one file in your query.

You can either let the system assign the file ID, or if it would help you remember the files better, you can type your own file ID. Leaving "*ID" as the value, as shown in Figure 5-4, defaults to the Query/400 assigning the name. Again, if you really want to specify your own file ID, you can make it from one to three characters. The first character must be alphabetic or $, #, or @. The last two characters in the file ID can be alphabetic, numeric, or $, #, or @..

That's about it for specifying files, until we hit the JOIN file case study in Chapter 19 of this QuikCourse. It's now time to finish up this file selection chapter.

Files for VENDORP Case Study

Once you type the file name (VENDORP) and the Library (HELLO), as shown in the panel in Figure 5-3, you are basically finished with the file selection for FIRSTQ. Just press ENTER to continue.

Query/400 obligingly returns the name of the format to the panel and replaces the *FIRST value with the name of the first file format, as shown in Figure 5-5.

Figure 5-5 Pick Your Files

```
                         Specify File Selections

Type choices, press Enter.  Press F9 to specify an additional
    file selection.

    File . . . . . . . . .   VENDORP      Name, F4 for list
       Library  . . . . . .    HELLO      Name, *LIBL, F4 for list
    Member . . . . . . . .   *FIRST       Name, *FIRST, F4 for list
    Format . . . . . . . .   VNDMSTR      Name, *FIRST, F4 for list




F3=Exit          F4=Prompt         F5=Report              F9=Add file
F12=Cancel       F13=Layout        F24=More keys
Select file(s), or press Enter to confirm.
```

Once you press ENTER, you have finished File Selection. You will then return to the Define the Query panel, as shown in Figure 5-6. You can now see the ">" sign, since you have completed your file selections.

Figure 5-6 Define The Query Panel

```
                            Define the Query
Query . . . . . . :    FIRSTQ            Option . . . . . :    CREATE
Library . . . . :      HELLO       CCSID . . . . . . . :      37
Type options, press Enter.  Press F21 to select all.
  1=Select

Opt    Query Definition Option
     > Specify file selections
       Define result fields
       Select and sequence fields
       Select records
       Select sort fields
       Select collating sequence
       Specify report column formatting
       Select report summary functions
       Define report breaks
       Select output type and output form
       Specify processing options

  F3=Exit          F5=Report          F12=Cancel
  F13=Layout       F18=Files          F21=Select all
```

You now have specified enough to have a complete file query on the VENDORP. If you ended your query now, and asked for it to run, you would get a report that contained every field in every record of the VENDORP file. Even if you chose not to end your query definition, by pressing F5, you could get the same report at your display session just to see what it would look like.

Neither of these options may be exactly what you want. The report may be too inclusive. You may want it to print. The data may not be shaped well. The spacing may be poor. The column headings may not be right, and there may be more columns or more records than you need or want. That's why the other options in the Define the Query prompt exist. Now it's time to learn how to use them.

And so, it's time to move on to the next menu option – Define Result Fields. We'll pick this up with Chapter 6 straight ahead. Now, we're starting to cook!

Chapter 6   Define Result Fields

Create a Result Field

The next option on the Define The Query panel, as shown in Figure
6-1, is to define result fields..

Figure 6-1 Define The Query - Results Fields

```
                       Define the Query
  Query . . . . . . :   FIRSTQ        Option . . . . . :    CREATE
  Library . . . . :     HELLO       CCSID . . . . . . :      37
  Type options, press Enter.  Press F21 to select all.
    1=Select

  Opt     Query Definition Option
  > Specify file selections
    1      Define result fields
           Select and sequence fields
           Select records
           Select sort fields
           Select collating sequence
           Specify report column formatting
           Select report summary functions
           Define report breaks
           Select output type and output form
           Specify processing options

    F3=Exit         F5=Report       F12=Cancel
    F13=Layout      F18=Files       F21=Select all
```

Notice that we have highlighted the selection of this option. Just
place a "1" by the Define Result Fields menu option, and press
ENTER. You will be taken to a panel similar to that in Figure 6-2.

Figure 6-2 Define Result Fields

```
                    Define Result Fields

Type definitions using field names or constants and operators,
press Enter.
Operators:  +,  , *, /, SUBSTR, ||, DATE...

Field       Expression                Column Heading    Len   Dec




                                                    Bottom

Field       Text                                    Len   Dec
VNDNBR      VENDOR NUMBER                              5    0
NAME        NAME                                      25
ADDR1       ADDRESS LINE 1                            25
CITY        CITY                                      15
                                                   More...
F3=Exit       F5=Report      F9=Insert    F11=Display names only
F12=Cancel    F13=Layout   F20=Reorganize   F24=More keys
```

The Objective

When you arrive at the Define Result Fields panel when creating a
query, it will be blank as in Figure 6-2. You will get to specify the
fields you wish to create. In this simple example, we want to create a
field, which holds the result of a calculation. The objective is to
calculate a 2% penalty on the BALOWE field, in case a payment is
made late. Figure 6-3 shows the Query/400 calculation.

Figure 6-3 Define Result Fields

```
                    Define Result Fields

Type definitions using field names or constants and operators,
press Enter.
Operators:  +,  , *, /, SUBSTR, ||, DATE...

Field       Expression                Column Heading    Len   Dec
PENLTY      BALOWE * .02              LATE               7    3
                                      PAYMENT
                                      PENALTY

                                                    Bottom

Field       Text                                    Len   Dec
VNDNBR      VENDOR NUMBER                              5    0
NAME        NAME                                      25
ADDR1       ADDRESS LINE 1                            25
CITY        CITY                                      15
                                                   More...
F3=Exit       F5=Report      F9=Insert    F11=Display names only
F12=Cancel    F13=Layout   F20=Reorganize   F24=More keys
```

The Coding for the Operation

As you can see in Figure 6-3, you can define a potential late penalty
by filling in the Define Result Filed panel as shown. The way you
define fields in Query/400 is quite simple.

Field Prompt

In the Field Prompt area of Figure 6-3, you specify the name of the
new field, which you are defining to the query. In this case, it is
"PENLTY." You make up the name for this field. The name cannot
exist in any of the database files which are part of the query. When
each record is read from the file(s) in the query, the calculation is
performed, and the results are stored in the field named in the Field
prompt.

Using the New Field

This field can then be used in other operations in the query. For
example, you can sort on this field, or you can perform a summary
function against the field in a subsequent Query menu option when
building the full Query definition.

Creating the Expression

The next prompt area contains the heading Expression. XIn the
Expression area , you use the fields from the database, which are
listed at the bottom of the panel, to calculate a result field for each
record. You can also use numeric constants, along with the database
fields, to complete your expressions. The expression portrayed in
Figure 6-3 is shown below for a quick analysis:

BALOWE * .02

Notice that this expression uses a field from the VENDORP database
file (BALOWE,) as well as a numeric constant (.02). The expression
says, "Multiply the balance owed, as stored in the BALOWE field by

2% represented in decimal form as .02, and store the result in the new field called PENLTY.. The "*" is computereeze, for multiply, since an X represents the letter "X."

BALOWE is not in the database field list at the bottom of Figure 6-3. For you to see this field definition in the database list, you would have to position the cursor to that area of the panel, and roll forward (twice) until you came to the area of the list, as shown in Figure 6-4.

Figure 6-4 Define Result Fields - BALOWE

```
                        Define Result Fields

Type definitions using field names or constants and operators,
press Enter.
Operators:  +,  , *, /, SUBSTR, ||, DATE...

Field      Expression                   Column Heading    Len   Dec
PENLTY     BALOWE * .02                  LATE                7     3
                                         PAYMENT
                                         PENALTY




                                                       Bottom

Field        Text                                     Len   Dec
BALOWE       BALANCE OWED                               9     2
SRVRTG       G=GOOD, A=AVERAGE, B=BAD, P=PREFERRED      1


                                                    More...
F3=Exit         F5=Report       F9=Insert    F11=Display names only
F12=Cancel      F13=Layout    F20=Reorganize    F24=More keys
```

Of course, if you know the field name, without having to see it in the list, you can certainly type it into your expression. However, it is a good practice to assure yourself that you have spelled it properly by checking it in the list.

If you are an application developer, the result field calculation in Figure 6-4 probably looks intuitive. If you are a user, it may or may not be obvious. The key part of the result field calculation is the expression area, and there is lots more to talk about in this area. We'll be right back to do exactly that, but first let's finish our discussion about the other prompts in this panel for the VENDORP database file case study.

Finding Your Query Fields

To help you find the fields in the database files, as noted above, Query/400 very nicely lists them at the bottom of this panel. In this way, you do not have to worry about what the fields look like in DDS or in the actual file object. The Query program formats and presents them for your convenience.

You can then use the Roll or Page Down / Up keys for more fields as needed. We had to do this above to find BALOWE, in Figure 6-4. To find a field in the list, position the cursor in the listed fields at the bottom of the panel, and press the Roll or Paging keys to go forward or backward through the list.

Column Headings

Now, let's move over to the next prompt heading, the Column Heading area. This is where you can supply the new result field with a column heading for use in this Query. Since the new field cannot be in the database, Query/400 cannot extract a database column heading for it. To put a fancy heading on the column, you can type the heading of your choice for this new value right here as you define your Query.

Length & Decimal Prompts

Move over one more column and you will find the Length (Len) column heading, followed by the Decimals (Dec) column heading.

In the Length area, if the field is numeric, you can choose to tell Query/400 just how big you want to make this new result field. For numeric fields, once you define a length, you must also use the next column (Dec) to specify the number of decimal places in the field. Use zero if there are no decimal places. If the length is specified, the decimal positions must also be specified.

Query Can Determine the Length

Query/400 will determine the length for each result field you define, if you leave the length (Len) field blank. This trick works for numeric and alphabetic fields. One drawback is that Query creates big sized fields. This may bother you if you are trying to mush a lot of information into your report. You may not want to clutter it with big fat columns. To help you in this regard, Query/400 provides a means by which you can check out the result field size, which Query has calculated for the field. Just press F13, and you will get a report layout, which will tell you the sizes of all the fields in your Query..

For alphabetic type fields, you have no choice. You may not specify the length of the result field. Don't worry! Query calculates its proper size. Though you can specify the length for numeric fields, you are not obliged to, and in most cases, you probably do not want to.

For numeric result fields, Query/400 automatically sets the length as the total number of digits in the field necessary to hold the maximum result. It includes the number of digits to the left and right of the decimal point, but not the decimal point itself.

Result Field in Case Study

In Figure 6-4, we defined the result field PENLTY, with a LEN of 7, and a DEC of 3. If we know that our data does not have any big fields, this may be OK. However, it may not. The BALOWE field is defined as LEN of 9 and DEC of 2. There are 7 whole numbers in this value. Leaving only four whole numbers (7, 3) in the result field may cause truncation of larger numbers.

Additionally, BALOWE has two decimals (9, 2). When this is multiplied by a two decimal constant value (.02), the result can have four decimal places. Thus, a LEN of 7 and a DEC of 3, instead of a DEC of 4, will sometimes result in the truncation of decimal precision.

Field Size Implications

Again, depending on how well you know your data, this can be a big mistake or no mistake at all. The point is that you can avoid this issue by not specifying a length (or decimal position) for alphabetic and numeric fields. You can let "George" do it. If you were to have left the LEN and DEC prompts blank for PENLTY, for example, Query/400 would have allocated a field at a LEN of 11 and DEC of 4.

In this way, there is no possibility of truncation of whole numbers or decimal precision. Yes, an (11, 4) field is quite large, and it may create formatting issues for you. If you are concerned about the amount of space it will take to print this calculated number in the report, you can adjust its column size for printing later using the Specify report column formatting option of the Define the Query menu. This option is covered in Chapter 11.

Advantages of Calculated Result Fields

The ability to define new fields on the fly is a very powerful Query feature. For example, you can take a quantity field, multiply it by price, and subtract a discount amount, to create a line extension field. You can then sort on this field, average it, or perform other powerful functions on it so that you can better satisfy the information demands of your organization.

The point, is that if a field can be calculated from existing fields, it does not have to be in the database to use it in your Query. By defining fields in this fashion, these new results are calculated "on the fly," as you execute your query. When you think about it, that is really something.

Types of Expressions

Now that we have completed the case study result field calculation for PENLTY, with all of the associated prompts, we have come back to the Expressions prompt to take a look at the types of calculations that you can use to create new fields or re-format existing fields. The five types of expressions we will examine are as follows:

1. Numeric Expressions
2. Character Expressions (Alphabetic and special characters)
3. Date Expressions
4. Time Expressions
5. Time Stamp Expressions

The last three expressions are all very similar in that they work with data with very specific formats. Date, Time, and Time Stamps are very tricky in QUERY/400, and these are considered advanced topics for most users. In many organizations, where users do their own queries, an IT person creates a model query with the calculated result fields for time/date. This saves new users the headaches of working from scratch in an area requiring more IT knowledge than a typical query.

These functions most often pertain to the conversion of an external field date format to an internal format or vice versa. A common example is to provide a character representation of a numeric value for a date, time, or timestamp function. When this is done, the date in the result field could then be used in a character expression, such as a concatenation and substring. Both concatenation and substring operations are explained below.

> ☐ Hint: Application developers refer to alphabetic fields as alphanumeric or character, because they can not only contain letters, but they can also contain numbers, special characters and symbols such as $,&, @, etc.

Help Available for Expressions

You can get lots of help if you want to deploy Date, Time, and Timestamp facilities. For example, Query/400 provides wonderful help text which enables you to determine how to perform many functions in the product. If you have a need to use any of the special functions, you can invoke context-sensitive Query help by positioning the cursor to the Expression area and pressing F1 or the Help key.

Additionally, the "Query Users Guide," offered by IBM from its documentation Web site is also very helpful. In Appendix A, we provide instructions for finding IBM manuals, such as the "Query User's Guide." Moreover, we include a nice Date example using the DIGITS function as well as a Current-Date function near the end of this chapter.

Detailed Look at Expressions

Let's start our description of expressions by first explaining the two most common forms of expressions in some detail – numeric and character. Then, we will introduce you to the other functions available in the Date, Time, and Timestamp areas.

Numeric Expressions

The operators used in numeric expressions and their meanings are as follows:

+	Addition
-	Subtraction
*	Multiplication
/	Division

From these simple operators, you can make some fairly complex calculations. We will now step outside the case study, until next chapter while we go over some detailed descriptions and examples.

Numeric Expression Examples

In the following examples, assume that QTY is equal to 10, QTY2 is equal to 2, U/M is equal to 5, and X is equal to 20. The results of the expressions below are shown on the right side.

Expression	Result
QTY	10
15	15
QTY + 15	25
15 + 35	50
15 + QTY	25
QTY + QTY2	12
QTY / UM	2
QTY * 3 * X	600

Operation Hierarchy & the Use of Parentheses

Of course, not all your calculations will be as simple as these examples. In fact, there may be times that you need to do more than one calculation in the same statement. When you do more than one calculation within a numeric expression, you can and probably should, use parentheses.

If you have attended math / algebra courses in your past, you know that the calculations within parentheses are always performed before those outside of parentheses. They help you control which operations occur first. Likewise, with parentheses, you tell Query/400 the order in which to perform calculations. As a side benefit, parentheses help make an expression easier to read and understand.

Of course, the order in which calculations are performed affects the result. If you use nested parentheses for example, 30 * (X - (Y + Z)), the calculations are done for the innermost parentheses first (in the example, Y + Z), then the next innermost pair, and so on.

If you do not use parentheses, the rule that Query/400 uses, is very simple: First comes multiplication and division, from left to right. Then comes addition and subtraction, again, from left to right. The following two examples demonstrate this notion:

1.   (7 + 2) * 2   equals 18
2.   7 + 2 * 2   equals 11

Character Expressions

Query/400 also provides four alphabetic operators / functions for character expressions. These are as follows:

Function	Description
| |	Concatenate
DIGITS	Digits Function
SUBSTR	Substring
VALUE	Value Function

DIGITS and VALUE

The DIGITS and VALUE functions come in handy when the input for your expression is not in the form needed for the operation. These are somewhat advanced for us at this time, but we will give each a shot, and we will provide an example. If this makes little sense for you now, you may want to earmark the page for a return trip.

These functions are also covered very nicely in the Query Users Guide, and there is a small amount of Help Text available under Expressions in the Define Result Fields panel.

The DIGITS function returns the character representation of a number, and the VALUE function returns the first not-null argument in a list (contains a value).

Simple Character Expressions

Before we describe these four character operations, just as a numeric expression could consist of a single field name or a single constant, so also can a character expression. In the three examples which follow, consider that NAME is equal to Bob, and ADDRES is equal to 11 Jones St. The field name in which the result of the expression is stored is RESULT. The below table shows the expression and the RESULT field.

Expression	RESULT
NAME	Bob
'11 Jones St.'	11 Jones St.
ADDRES	11 Jones St.

A key point to consider with character constants, which are also called literals, is that they are defined in expressions within quotes. If a string of characters is given with no quotes, Query/400 assumes it is a field name.

You can see above that the RESULT field value is "Bob," when the expression contains the field named NAME, and NAME contains the value, "Bob." When a literal is used in the expression, such as '11 Jones St.' the RESULT is "11 Jones St.," and when the field name ADDRES is the entire expression, the RESULT field takes on the value of the expression, which is "11 Jones St."

Concatenation Expressions

Concatenation means bringing two or more text fields and / or text constant values together into one result field. The general form of the concatenation expression is as follows:

value1 || value 2 || value 3 . . .

The fancy || bars are the symbols for the concatenation operation.

Concatenation Examples

Consider that NAM is equal to Bob and that LAST is equal to Jones.

Expression	Result
NAM || LAST	BobJones
NAM || 'Jones'	BobJones
'Bob' || ' ' || LAST	Bob Jones

In the first example, the value "Bob," from NAM, is concatenated with the value "Jones" from LAST. The next example shows the value "Bob," from NAM, being concatenated with the literal value 'Jones.' You may notice that in the first two results, there is no space between the first and last names. In the last example, the literal value "Bob" is concatenated with the literal value of one blank space and then again with the value "Jones" from LAST. Notice that the last result has a separation between the first and last name.

DIGITS Character Expressions

The DIGITS function returns a character representation of a number. The form is:

DIGITS (expression)

The expression argument must be an integer or decimal value. The result of the function is a fixed length character string. The result is a string of digits (0 through 9,) that represents the absolute value of the argument, without regard to its scale. The result of this function does not include a sign or a decimal point. However, the result does include any necessary leading zeros.

Because the DIGITS operation can be used against numbers in other than simple decimal format, the following information regarding the result length is given for your consideration:

The length of the return string is:

5   If the argument is a small binary value with no decimal positions.

10 If the argument is a large binary value with no decimal positions.

Why Use DIGITS Function?

Why would you use DIGITS? As a Query user, you may find that
the data is not always the way it should be for your use. Though the
right thing for IT to do, if this is the case, is to give you better shaped
data by building a simple data warehouse, the burden of data
determination and use is often left to the Query user.

DIGITS Example

Suppose, for example, that to handle the Y2K problem, your
company changed the type of its six position, numeric date fields, to
packed decimal. The date had been taken 6 positions in the record
and was unpacked. It was of the form yy/mm/dd   (e.g. 02/10/22).
By changing the type of the field, they were able to change the date
format to mm/dd/yyyy (08/02/2002). Instead of 6 digits in 6
positions, packing the field gave them 11 digits in the same space.

In simple terms, they pack the data, so that 11 digits could be stored
in the six positions available. Without getting technical, let's say they
created a packed numeric field and called it NEWDAT. Since this
new date only needs 8 positions in the new format, the first three
positions of NEWDAT would always contain zeroes.

For your DIGITS Query example, let's say you need the data from
just the current year (2002.) How do you get it? YEAR is not one of
the fields in the database record.

Right! You first use the DIGITS function. It goes like this:

RESDAT DIGITS(NEWDAT)

The end result of the DIGITS function applied against the
NEWDAT field would be a character string in the format:

'000mmddyyyy'

'00008022002'

So, now that the DIGITS operation has transformed this numeric data to a character string and has stored it in RESDAT, you can segregate the year component into another result field, called YR. To do this, use the Substring operation which we are just about to explain. For now, let us make note that the year begins in the eighth position of RESDAT and that it is four characters long. Check the substring examples for the answer.

Substring Character Expressions

Substring is the opposite of concatenate. Whereas concatenate takes two or more things and combines them into one big thing, substring takes a big thing and makes smaller pieces from it. As a point of note, to create two pieces that had previously been combined through concatenation, you would require two substring operations. The form of the SUBSTR operation is as follows:

SUBSTR(value, offset, length)

This says to go grab a piece of the field name, or the constant, before the first comma (value), starting in the position specified by the second parameter (offset), for a length of whatever is specified in the third parameter (length). First, we solve the DIGITS example from above, and then we have a few other examples for you to absorb. Additionally, in the DIGITS example, the second example extracts the month. For the other examples below, remember that NAM1 = BobJones and NAM2 = Bob Jones. In case you missed the subtlety, the second "Bob Jones" has a space between the names.

Expression	Result
SUBSTR(RESDAT, 8, 4)	2002
SUBSTR(RESDAT, 1, 2)	08
SUBSTR(NAM1, 1, 3)	Bob
SUBSTR(NAM1, 4, 4)	Jone
SUBSTR(NAM2, 3, 4)	b Jo
SUBSTR('AB',1, (2-1))	A

In the above example, the expressions are reasonably easy to read. Let's say the result field for expression 1 is YR, expression 2 is MO, and expressions 3 to 6 are N.AM3. At the end of each expression above, the value under result would be stored in the respective result field - YR, MO, or NAM3. Take a look at each expression above, and assure yourself that it makes sense before you move on.

One more piece of information may be helpful when you begin creating advanced queries. The Length parameter may be provided by a field or another expression. This is shown in the sixth example above (two minus 1.)

VALUE Character Expressions

The VALUE function can be used in any type of expression: character, numeric, date, time, or timestamp. Using the form, VALUE(X, Y), it returns the first not-null argument in a string. The arguments (fields) are evaluated in the order in which they are specified. They must be compatible. Character string arguments, for example, are not compatible with numbers.

Assume that the result of the function is to be stored in a field named ANSWER. In the VALUE function format above, "X" is a field, and "Y" can be a field. "Y" can be a value, or a list of fields or values. "X" can be any data type, and may be a previously-defined result field or any database file field. The result of the operation, which is stored in ANSWER, can be null only if all arguments can be null. In this example, as you can see, we are hoping for a not null value. Therefore the ANSWER field should contain something that is zero or above.

VALUE Function Example

ANSWER VALUE(SALES, COST, 0)

In this example, if SALES and COST are null, the result stored in
ANSWER is 0. If SALES is null, and COST is 234, the value in
ANSWER is 234. If SALES is 334, and COST is 234, the value in
ANSWER is 334.

Date Expressions

There is a third kind of expression known as a Date Expression. It
performs an operation on a date. Date expressions can contain the
following operators or functions:

+   **(Addition)**
-                   **(Subtraction)**
CHAR
DATE
DAY
DAYS
MONTH
YEAR

Additional Date Information

Working with Dates, Times, and Time Stamps can get tricky, as we
have said repeatedly. There are a few things that can help you
understand what this is all about. In the paragraphs immediately
following, and in the example following Timestamp, we offer an
explanation of internal dates and date formatting with Query/400.

Though Time and Timestamp functions are not 100% analogous to Dates, the Date example shows similar logic to time, and timestamp, and can therefore be used as a model for all three. The choice of date is obvious. There are few ad hoc queries that do not rely on a date of some kind to narrow their scope.

AS/400 Date Format

First of all, the AS/400 has its own internal date format that is just six characters. It can deliver accurate dates from 1940 to 2039. Thus, if the AS/400's two-digit year format is used in a query, the range of displayed dates is limited to the 1940 through 2039 range. Though this is arbitrary, it is the way it is.

Any year from 40 through 99 is assumed to have a century of 19. Any year from 00 through 39 is assumed to have a century of 20. That's how IBM solved part of the Y2K problem with the AS/400 system. If a value outside of that range is in a field with a two-digit year format, it will be shown on a report as "+s." The AS/400 functions cannot materialize it. Therefore, IBM's recommendation is to use the CHAR function on that field specifying an SAA date format, and then select the result field for the report.

SAA Date Format (ISO, USA, etc)

Whoa, you may say! What is SAA? Let's just say that one of the things that IBM defined with SAA was the various date formats used across the world. You can use any of them, if it is appropriate for your work. These are shown in the following table:

International Standards Organization

ISO
yyyy mm dd
2002-10-22

IBM USA Standard

USA
mm/dd/yyyy
10/22/2002

IBM European Standard

EUR
dd.mm.yyyy
10.02.2002

Japanese Industrial Standard Christian era

JIS
yyyy-mm-dd
2002-10-22

In the example below, following Timestamp, we use the ISO format to bring the internal date to a character format, so that we can compare it with a database date.

Time Expressions

Before we get to the Date example below, there is a fourth type of expression called a Time Expression that we will now explore. This performs an operation on a time. Time expressions can contain the following operators or functions:

+   **Addition**
-   **Subtraction**
CHAR
TIME
HOUR
MINUTE
SECOND
MICROSECOND

Time Stamp Expressions

There is one more expression type. It is the fifth type of expression, and it is called a Timestamp Expression. It performs an operation on a timestamp. Timestamp expressions can contain the following operators or functions:

+   **Addition**
-   **Subtraction**
CHAR
TIMESTAMP

If you need to use the Date, Time and TimeStamp operations, they are located in the "IBM Query Users' Guide." You can use Appendix A in the back of this book to help find IBM manuals on the Web.

Current Date Example

Though it is very difficult to simplify the volumes of rules regarding date and time type fields, rather than just send you to the manual, we provide two valuable examples below.

Date / Time Example 1

You may have a need to capture the current date in a Query definition. To do this, you can use the expression

CDATE   Current(Date)

You probably would do this so that you could compare this date with a character date from your database for selection purposes. In this case, you would covert this date using the CHAR function, or perhaps DIGITS, to make the comparison.

Yesterday Date Example

You may also have a need to compare yesterday's date, with a date in your file. This can also be gained using the Current Date Function but you have to add the Days function, so that you can perform a little subtraction from the current date.

So, let's first derive yesterday's date with the Query/400 "Result Fields" facility. The Days function, as noted above, is necessary for your expression to accomplish its goal. This function converts a date to a number of days since a fixed date, as defined by IBM. (This date may be the beginning of recorded time or an arbitrary IBM-selected date.)

Using the Days function, you convert the current date to a number of days. Then, using date arithmetic, you subtract 1 from the Days function value. This gives the number of days for yesterday compared to IBM's defined base date. Now that the value is in days, you can use the Query/400 Date function to convert this number of days back to a real date. The value converts to yesterday's date in internal system date format.

In the example below, we use a single, nested expression to derive yesterday's date, and store it in the YDAY field.

YDAY Date(Days(Current(Date)) - 1)

Working from the innermost parentheses out, this uses the Current function to get the current date. The days function converts this to a value, say 50001, and then the -1 subtracts from the value to give 50000, which is converted back to a date one day less than the current date, using the Date function against the outside pair of parentheses.

Converting Yesterday to Character

Once you get yesterday's date, you convert it to a character date to compare against the date in your database, for record selection.

Using CHAR Function

You may recall in a prior example, we used the DIGITS function to change a database date to a character date. In this example, we want to change YDAY, which represents yesterday's date, stored in the internal date format, to character format. In this way, you can compare it against another database date (DBDAT), which is already stored in character form in the same format as ISO (yyyy mm dd).

I would bet you are about to conclude that the rhetoric is far greater than the function required for the task. In order to convert yesterday's date to character so that it can be compared, use the CHAR function as follows:

CMPDAT   CHAR(YDAY, ISO))

This takes the YDAY field, which contains the internal representation of yesterday's date, and makes a ten position character field from it, called CMPDAT. Later CMPDAT will be used to select records in the file. Though we have not covered that menu option yet, the Select Record test would look like this:

DBDAT EQ CMPDAT

As each DB record is read, the DBDAT field is compared to the CMPDAT field. Any record in the database, in which the DBDAT field contains yesterday's date, is selected for the query report. That's that!

Wrapping It Up

When you have finished defining all of your expressions, hit the ENTER key, and you come back to the Define the Query panel, as shown in Figure I-19. Notice there are now two areas checked as completed (">").

Figure 6-5 Define The Query - Result Fields

```
                       Define the Query
Query . . . . . . :    FIRSTQ           Option  . . . . . :    CREATE
Library . . . . :      HELLO            CCSID . . . . . . :    37
  Type options, press Enter.  Press F21 to select all.
    1=Select

  Opt    Query Definition Option
        > Specify file selections
        > Define result fields
          Select and sequence fields
          Select records
          Select sort fields
          Select collating sequence
          Specify report column formatting
          Select report summary functions
          Define report breaks
          Select output type and output form
          Specify processing options

  F3=Exit          F5=Report         F12=Cancel
  F13=Layout       F18=Files         F21=Select all
```

When building query definitions, users often get a sample of their wares as they progress through the query build. Now that the BALOWE result filed is defined and you are back to the Define the Query menu, it may be a good time to see if this result field has been calculated correctly. Just press F5, to get an intermediate report to your display. Check the value to be sure it is correct. If it is not correct, go back in and correct it. If it is right, it's time to move to Chapter 7, to select and sequence your fields.

Chapter 7. Select and Sequence Fields

Picking the Report Fields

The next stop on your Query journey is to move down one more item on the Define The Query panel, as shown in Figure 7-1.

Figure 7-1 Define The Query - Select Fields

```
                        Define the Query
  Query . . . . . . :    FIRSTQ         Option . . . . . :    CREATE
  Library . . . . :    HELLO          CCSID . . . . . . :    37
  Type options, press Enter.  Press F21 to select all.
    1=Select

  Opt     Query Definition Option
        > Specify file selections
        > Define result fields
    1     Select and sequence fields
          Select records
          Select sort fields
          Select collating sequence
          Specify report column formatting
          Select report summary functions
          Define report breaks
          Select output type and output form
          Specify processing options

   F3=Exit          F5=Report          F12=Cancel
  F13=Layout        F18=Files          F21=Select all
```

This time, we arrive at Select and Sequence Fields. When your panel looks like that in Figure 7-1, press the ENTER key. You'll be taken to the panel in Figure 7-2, which shows how to select fields and sequence fields for reporting.

Figure 7-2 Select and Sequence Fields

```
                       Select and Sequence Fields

Type sequence number (0 9999) for the names of up to 500 fields to
appear in the report, press Enter.

Seq   Field         Text                                     Len   Dec
9     PENLTY        BALOWE*.02                                 7     3
2     VNDNBR        VENDOR NUMBER                              5     0
1     NAME          NAME                                      25
3     ADDR1         ADDRESS LINE 1                            25
4     CITY          CITY                                      15
5     STATE         STATE                                      2
6     ZIPCD         ZIP'CODE                                   5     0
7     VNDCLS        VENDOR CLASS                               2     0
      VNDSTS        A=ACTIVE, D=DELETE, S=SUSPEND              1
8     BALOWE        BALANCE OWED                               9     2
      SRVRTG        G=GOOD, A=AVERAGE, B=BAD, P=PREFERRED      1


F3=Exit            F5=Report      F11=Display names only    F12=Cancel
F13=Layout         F20=Renumber   F21=Select all         F24=More keys
```

Sequence and Select

As you can see in Figure 7-2, selection and ordering of fields is as easy as placing a sequence number for the order of fields to be displayed.

The number does more than merely select a field to be on the Query report. It corresponds to how the fields will line up from left, to right on the report. Only those fields that have a number next to them are selected. Fields with no number do not appear in the query. In the sample shown in Figure 7-2, Accounting Code and Service Rating are not selected, and are therefore excluded from the report. PENLTY, the result field that we created in Chapter 6, is selected for the report as sequence # 9. It will print on the report as the rightmost column.

Rearrange Your Data

Again, the number is very important, since it corresponds to the order in which the fields will be displayed. Notice that you can use a different sequence number than the physical order of the fields on the Select and Sequence Fields screen. This has the effect of rearranging fields for the report.

When you hit ENTER on this panel, QUERY/400 will re-sequence the lines, put all of the ordered fields on top, and put the unused fields on the bottom. When you hit ENTER, your display should look like that in Figure 7-3.

Figure 7-3 Select and Sequence Fields - Resequenced

```
                       Select and Sequence Fields

   Type sequence number (0 9999) for the names of up to 500 fields to
   appear in the report, press Enter.

   Seq   Field         Text                                 Len  Dec

   1     NAME          NAME                                  25
   2     VNDNBR        VENDOR NUMBER                          5    0
   3     ADDR1         ADDRESS LINE 1                        25
   4     CITY          CITY                                  15
   5     STATE         STATE                                  2
   6     ZIPCD         ZIP'CODE                               5    0
   7     VNDCLS        VENDOR CLASS                           2    0
   8     BALOWE        BALANCE OWED                           9    2
   9     PENLTY        BALOWE*.02                             7    3
         VNDSTS        A=ACTIVE, D=DELETE, S=SUSPEND          1
         SRVRTG        G=GOOD, A=AVERAGE, B=BAD, P=PREFERRED  1



   F3=Exit        F5=Report      F11=Display names only    F12=Cancel
   F13=Layout     F20=Renumber   F21=Select all        F24=More keys
```

Make Some Changes

Before you return to the Define the Query panel in this case study, change the sequence back to having the Vendor Number field precede the Name field. Of course, it would be easier to do this if you had 10 between each sequence number, instead of 1. All you'd have to do is make is make VNDNBR a five and press ENTER. Of course, you could also end the job and come back in to this query. Query/400 will change the spacing to 10 automatically for you.

The case study examples are structured to accommodate the changed order. Make the change and press ENTER. Your panel should now look like that in Figure 7-4

Figure 7-4 Select and Sequence Fields - Corrected

```
                        Select and Sequence Fields

Type sequence number (0 9999) for the names of up to 500 fields to
appear in the report, press Enter.

Seq   Field           Text                              Len   Dec
1     VNDNBR          VENDOR NUMBER                       5     0
2     NAME            NAME                               25
3     ADDR1           ADDRESS LINE 1                     25
4     CITY            CITY                               15
5     STATE           STATE                               2
6     ZIPCD           ZIP'CODE                            5     0
7     VNDCLS          VENDOR CLASS                        2     0
8     BALOWE          BALANCE OWED                        9     2
9     PENLTY          BALOWE*.02                          7     3
      VNDSTS          A=ACTIVE, D=DELETE, S=SUSPEND       1
      SRVRTG          G=GOOD, A=AVERAGE, B=BAD, P=PREFERRED  1


F3=Exit          F5=Report      F11=Display names only    F12=Cancel
F13=Layout       F20=Renumber   F21=Select all        F24=More keys
```

See Report Anytime

As noted previously, at any point, you can hit F5 to get an intermediate, ad-hoc look at how well your query will execute. Feel free, as you are building your query, to hit the F5 key as long as you do not have exceedingly large files. F5 only hurts performance when the files are extremely large. If you are a user and not an IT developer, you should ask your IT folks which files might be a problem for you.

More Options

There are some other options on the Select and Sequence Fields panel that you should examine. If you press F11, for example, the text and the length information disappear, and more fields can fit on the screen in their place. When you learn your field names, and there are lots of fields, this is a good option to remember.

Command Keys

Before we move on, let's stop to take a look at the command keys and what they do for you. As in all IBM utilities, F3 ends the job. In

Query/400, along the way, it also asks if you want to save and/or run the query. F12 cancels what you have done and returns you to the Define the Query Panel. F13, as we have seen gives, you the left to right report layout, without running the query. F5, of course, runs the query to the display.

Renumber at Last

Pressing the F20 key renumbers the active fields, separating them by 10. Hey, we could have used this before, right? This helps when you choose to add a field. Just renumber the field(s), and then pick a number in between two fields for your insert.

Select All Fields

For the person who wants all fields selected, both manufactured fields such as PENLTY, and database fields such as VNDNBR, just press F21. Query/400 will place numbers, separated by 10, in all the fields as it selects them. You can then deselect or re-sequence as you choose. When you press ENTER, any field marked by you, or by the system, is selected.

So, let's say we press ENTER now and go back to the Define the Query panel. It will look like the display as shown in Figure 7-5.

Figure 7-5 Define The Query - Select Fields Completed

```
                          Define the Query
Query . . . . . . :   FIRSTQ           Option  . . . . . :    CREATE
Library . . . . :     HELLO            CCSID . . . . . . :      37
Type options, press Enter.  Press F21 to select all.
  1=Select

Opt    Query Definition Option
      > Specify file selections
      > Define result fields
      > Select and sequence fields
        Select records
        Select sort fields
        Select collating sequence
        Specify report column formatting
        Select report summary functions
        Define report breaks
        Select output type and output form
        Specify processing options


 F3=Exit          F5=Report        F12=Cancel
 F13=Layout       F18=Files        F21=Select all
```

Finished Is Good

Notice in Figure 7-5 that the finished mark ">" is now next to the third menu option since we have probably completed it. Though it looks complete, we can go back in to any option, after Query/400 marks it complete, either now ,or later by placing a "1" next to the option and pressing ENTER.

A Second Look

If you re-selected the Select and Sequence Fields option now, for example, you would see that Query/400 does not remember the numbers you placed by the fields, but, it does remember the sequence you placed them in. So, if you place a "1" again for Select and Sequence Fields, and you press ENTER, you will see the panel, as in Figure 7-6.

Figure 7-6 Select and Sequence Fields - Re-sequenced

```
                        Select and Sequence Fields

Type sequence number (0 9999) for the names of up to 500 fields to
appear in the report, press Enter.

Seq   Field           Text                                  Len  Dec
10    VNDNBR          VENDOR NUMBER                          5    0
20    NAME            NAME                                   25
30    ADDR1           ADDRESS LINE 1                         25
40    CITY            CITY                                   15
50    STATE           STATE                                   2
60    ZIPCD           ZIP'CODE                                5    0
70    VNDCLS          VENDOR CLASS                            2    0
80    BALOWE          BALANCE OWED                            9    2
90    PENLTY          BALOWE*.02                              7    3
      VNDSTS          A=ACTIVE, D=DELETE, S=SUSPEND           1
      SRVRTG          G=GOOD, A=AVERAGE, B=BAD, P=PREFERRED   1


F3=Exit          F5=Report      F11=Display names only    F12=Cancel
F13=Layout       F20=Renumber   F21=Select all           F24=More keys
```

When you hit ENTER, you will return to the Define the Query panel
as in Figure 7-5. Then, you are ready for Record Selection as you
will find in Chapter 8.

Chapter 8.   Select Records

It's Getting Interesting

Now that you have all of your fields selected, including the newly calculated PENLTY result field, you can move down the Define the Query panel, as shown in Figure 8-1, one more line to select the records that you want to be included in this query.

Figure 8-1 Define The Query - Select Records

```
                          Define the Query
Query . . . . . . :     FIRSTQ            Option . . . . . :     CREATE
Library . . . . :      HELLO         CCSID . . . . . . :     37
Type options, press Enter.  Press F21 to select all.
  1=Select

Opt     Query Definition Option
      > Specify file selections
      > Define result fields
      > Select and sequence fields
  1     Select records
        Select sort fields
        Select collating sequence
        Specify report column formatting
        Select report summary functions
        Define report breaks
        Select output type and output form
        Specify processing options

  F3=Exit           F5=Report        F12=Cancel
  F13=Layout        F18=Files        F21=Select all
```

When you place a "1" at this option and press ENTER, you come to the Select Records panel, as shown in Figure 8-2.

Figure 8-2 AS/400 Query Select Records Panel

```
                         Select Records

Type comparisons, press Enter.  Specify OR to start each new group.
  Tests:  EQ, NE, LE, GE, LT, GT, RANGE, LIST, and LIKE

AND/OR  Field          Test   Value (Field, Number, or'Characters')
  ___     _____          ___    _____
  ___     _____          ___    _____
  ___     _____          ___    _____
  ___     _____          ___    _____
  ___     _____          ___    _____


Field               Field
VNDNVR              ZIPCD
NAME                VNDCLS
ADDR1               VNDSTS
CITY                BALOWE
STATE               SRVRTG


Bottom
  F3=Exit         F5=Report        F9=Insert         F11=Display text
  F12=Cancel      F13=Layout       F20=Reorganize    F24=More keys
```

What do you think your report would look like if you hit F5 right now? What purpose would this serve? Well, if you pressed F5 right now, you could find out, among other things, how many records there are in the query report, when no record selection is done. There should be as many records as exist in the database file. Of course, you would also get a first glimpse of the report itself, its formatting, and its contents.

Look At the Report

What value does this have? Let's say that you find that there are 17 records in the VENDORP file by rolling through Query screens, which hold 14 records each. If you select records based upon your particular criteria which should, by definition, exclude certain records from the report and include others, there should be less than 17 records in the Select Records report. If the total number of records selected is still 17, then you can be pretty sure that you made a mistake in forming your selection test.

☐ Caution: If there are millions of records in the file instead of just a couple, as there are at a number of my consulting accounts, such as Klein Candy in WIlkes-Barre, it goes without saying that this is a poor testing method for those particular files. You'll be waiting quite a while for something to come back to the screen panel, and you will create unacceptable system performance.

Let's take a look at what our Query report would look like if you did exactly what I suggested above. The result is in Figure 8-3 below.

Figure 8-3 AS/400 Query Report - All Records

```
                        Display Report
                                    Report width  . . . . . :      130
  Position to line  . . . . .       Shift to column  . . . . .
  Line    ....+....1....+....2....+....3....+....4....+....5....+....6....+....7..
          NAME                      VENDOR   ADDRESS LINE 1           CITY
                                    NUMBER

  000001 J B COMPANY                    38   3817 N. PULASKI          SCRANTON
  000002 SCRANTON INC                   40   2147 S MAIN ST           OLD FORGE
  000003 PASS PAX INC                   42   1539 OAK HILL            OLD FORGE
  000004 J B EQUIP INC                  44   2232 FOUEST              SCRANTON
  000005 K D BUTTS WALLACE INC          46   2150 TOUGHY              SCRANTON
  000006 DENTON AND BALL                48   7934 S SCRANTON AVE      SCRANTON
  000007 JOHN STUDIOS                   49   2040 N BELTWAY           SCRANTON
  000008 A MACHINE CORP.                25   1345 Prill Avenue        Chicago
  000009 B MACHINERY                    26   45 Ginzo Lane            Wokegon
  000010 C ENGRAVING CO                 28   Pedulllion Avenue        Greghert
  000011 D CONTROLS                     30   45 Fognetta Place        Kernstin
  000012 I POWER EQUIPMENT              32   56 Fineel La             Swingder
  000013 ROBIN   COMPANY                34   11 Robin Lane            Robin
  000014 F STEEL CO                     36   78 Engraved Rd.          Mattusic
                                                                     More...


  000015 Bird Bath House               52   39 Seedy Lane            Tena Hoop
  000016 Feenala Grund Mfg.            56   765 Neophite Blvd         Castigoga
  000017 Thinking Clocks               10   43 Timestamp Rd          Gultimo

   F3=Exit      F12=Cancel     F19=Left      F20=Right      F21=Split
```

Stretching the F5 Results Panel

As you can probably tell, only 14 lines of Query fit on the default panel size. However, the whole report is in memory. You get the rest by rolling forward through the display. In this case, there are just 17 records in the file in no apparent sequence. The last three records show up because I cut and pasted them into this panel shot to make it easier to see the three records that would appear after one roll. Thus, in this case, it takes you one roll to know how many records are in

the file. I grant you that for most real files that you use, you'll be
rolling quite a while longer.

Selection Operators

Most of the hints that you need to do well with the Select Records
panel, are visible at the top of the panel. They are included right
under the Select Records panel title. You choose one of these
operators and you plug it right under the test prompt on the line you
are going to use for testing. This determines the type of test you are
telling Query/400 to perform on each record that it reads from the
file(s), to determine if the record makes the report.

If you do not want all records, the Select records panel is your ticket
to getting just the records you want. You pick the ones you want. In
Figure I-29, you see that the VENDORP case study query is set to
select just those records whose balance owed is greater than $400.00.
On the top of the panel you can see the other operators that you can
use for selection besides the greater than GT test. The list of selection
verbs is as follows:

Op Code Type of Test

Op Code	Type of Test
EQ	Equal
NE	Not Equal
LE	Less than or Equal
GE	Greater than or Equal
LT	Less than
GT	Greater than
RANGE	Is the value in a range?
LIST	Is the value in a list?
LIKE	Is the value like, nut not the same as, the comparison
value	

Combining Operators

All of these operators can be used to select records in queries. Valid operations can also be ORed and ANDed together (logical "OR" and logical "AND") to form even more complex selection criteria.

Value Prompt

The columns on the selection statement other than Test are mostly self explanatory. Moving from the Test column, to the right on the display in Figure 7-2, you find the value that you are testing for under the heading, Value. When you enter a selection test, this will be the area in which you specify the value against which you are comparing.

The value column can support any of the following:

field name
numeric constant
SBCS constant   *
DBCS only constant   **
DBCS open constant   **
DBCS graphic constant **
date constant   ***
time constant   ***
timestamp constant   ***
list of values
pattern value

*   a.k.a - normal character constant
**   double byte character set – not covered in this book.
***   Date and time type constants - not covered in this book.

Specifying the Field to Be Tested

For each of your selection tests, you type the value to be compared in the "Value" area of the selection line. The value is compared against a selected field from the database as records are read. The database field is specified under the heading "Field." The contents of the field named in this area are tested against the contents of Value — as each record is read. There may be one value or a list of values, depending on the type of operation. The result of the test determines whether that record is selected for the Query report.

Field Name Prompt

For each comparison test, you type the name of the field to be tested in this Field prompt area. You can use only field names that are in the list in the lower part of this display. These are listed on the bottom of the panel for your convenience. You can scroll through them to assure that you have the correct spelling, but you must type the value into the selection statement. You cannot just move the cursor, and have it appear.

Having the field names right in front of you is a handy reminder to help assure that you will select all fields that apply. Of course, if the Query/400 application were cursor or mouse driven, the process could be made even easier by having the selection of a field cause its inclusion on the selection line. For now, and possibly for eternity, that may be just my wishful thinking. Let IBM know how you feel about that.

And / Or Prompt

Moving to the very beginning of the statement line (left side) from the Value area, you come to the AND/OR prompt. Whenever you specify a second line for selections the AND/OR line becomes operative. You must specify whether both conditions must be true for the record to be selected. For this, use "AND." If just one condition must be true for the record to be selected, use "OR."

It is virtually impossible to create a complex query without AND and / or OR statements. You use the AND and OR values, as needed, between your pairs of comparison tests. These indicate how the comparisons are to be related and grouped.

You would leave the AND / OR column blank if you define only one comparison for a query, as in the VENDORP example below.

And / Or Rules

The logic behind these values is as follows: An AND value indicates that the pair of tests must both be true before the results of the AND can be true. An OR value indicates that only one of the tests needs to be true for the results of the OR to be true.

For each pair of comparisons, Query/400 assumes an AND value if you do not specify one for the comparison test. To repeat, a blank column separating two selections is not meaningless. It is the same as an AND condition. Having said that, it is recommended to always code values so that assumptions about defaults are not mis-applied.

If no ORs are specified, only records that meet each and every defined comparison test (selection statements) are selected for the query. If your query is satisfied when just one of the tests is true, then make sure that you specify ORs to connect each one of the tests.

And / Or Query Processing

When you use both ANDs and ORs, it gets tricky and begins to hurt your head a little. Keep this in mind. It will help. Each OR separates groups of comparisons connected by ANDs. Starting from the first comparison test, if the results of all the AND comparisons done before an OR statement are all true, Query stops comparing and selects that record. The OR is satisfied when all the ANDS preceding it are true.

If the test results are not all true, Query continues comparing the next group of ANDs, and so on, and so on until there are no more ORs. We may also say that whenever a group of AND comparisons are all true, regardless of which side of the OR statement they are on (top or bottom), the record is selected. If one part of each of the ANDs is false, the record is not to be selected.

Working the Query with Selections

The reason that IBM built a Select Records facility into the Query/400 product is that you may not want to see all of the records in the file(s). That is the case with the VENDORP file. Let's say that you just want to see those records whose balance field is greater than $400.00. To do this, you would construct a test, to include records only when the BALOWE field is greater than 400.00. The full Query/400 selection statement to achieve this would look as follows.

AND/OR	Field	Test Value
BALOWE	**GT**	**400.00**

With this statement, you are telling Query/400 to include a record in the Query report, whenever the Balance field (BALOWE) is greater than (GT) four hundred dollars (400.00). If you placed this selection line within your query, it would look very similar to the panel in Figure 8-4. (I-29)

Figure 8-4 AS/400 Query Select Records Panel

```
                         Select Records

    Type comparisons, press Enter.  Specify OR to start each new group.
       Tests:  EQ, NE, LE, GE, LT, GT, RANGE, LIST, and LIKE

    AND/OR  Field            Test   Value (Field, Number, or'Characters')
      ___    BALOWE_____      GT___   400.00  _____
      ___    _____        ___     _____
      ___    _____        ___     _____
      ___    _____        ___     _____
      ___    _____        ___     _____


    Field              Field
    VNDNVR             ZIPCD
    NAME               VNDCLS
    ADDR1              VNDSTS
    CITY               BALOWE
    STATE              SRVRTG

    Bottom
    F3=Exit          F5=Report        F9=Insert        F11=Display text
    F12=Cancel       F13=Layout       F20=Reorganize   F24=More keys
```

Describing the Sample Select

The example shown in Figure 7-4 is very simple. You remember what it says from above. It says that a record will be selected if the balance owed is greater than $400.00. I would expect that a reasonable number of the records, in the VENDORP file have balances above $400.00. Thus, you should have a nice report of VENDORP records included in any of your queries which depend on this Selection definition. In fact, if we were to hit F5 after typing in the selection statement, the report would look like the panel in Figure 8-5.

Figure 8-5 AS/400 Query Report - Selected Records

```
                        Display Report
                              Report width . . . . . :
130
  Position to line  . . . . .          Shift to column  . . . . . .
  Line
  ....+....1....+....2....+....3....+....4....+....5....+....6....+....7..
          NAME                   VENDOR   ADDRESS LINE 1            CITY
                                 NUMBER

000001 K D BUTTS WALLACE INC       46    2150 TOUGHY
SCRANTON
000002 DENTON AND BALL             48    7934 S SCRANTON AVE
SCRANTON
000003 A MACHINE CORP.             25    1345 Prill Avenue        Chicago
000004 B MACHINERY                 26    45 Ginzo Lane            Wokegon
000005 D CONTROLS                  30    45 Fognetta Place
Kernstin
000006 Feenala Grund Mfg.          56    765 Neophite Blvd
Castigoga
000007 Thinking Clocks             10    43 Timestamp Rd          Gottime
****** ********  End of report   ********

  F3=Exit      F12=Cancel      F19=Left      F20=Right      F21=Split
```

Scrolling Right and Left

As you can see in the panel shown in Figure 8-5, there are seven records with balances over $400.00. However, the F5 report is too wide for the display. Therefore, it is truncated on the right. If you look at the bottom of the panel shown in Figure 8-5, you can see that there are two function keys which change the window on the display. To see areas of the display that are truncated on the right, press F20 until you see the column you want. To see areas of the display that are truncated on the left, press F19 until you are back to position 1 of the report.

From the panel shown in Figure 8-5, for you to see the BALOWE field, then, you would need to hit the F20 key (shift + F8) one time. You would then see a panel such as that shown in Figure 8-6.

Figure 8-6 AS/400 Query Report - Selection Right View

```
                              Display Report
                                        Report width . . . . . . :
130
 Position to line  . . . . .              Shift to column  . . . . . .
 Line
 ....+....1....+....2....+....3....+....4....+....5....+....6....+....7..
            CITY            STATE  ZIP CODE  VENDOR      BALANCE     LATE
                                             CLASS       OWED
PAYMENT

PENALTY
000001      SCRANTON        PA     18,503    30            500.00
10.000
000002      SCRANTON        PA     18,504    20          3,500.00
70.000
000003      Chicago         IL     45,903    10          7,500.00
150.000
000004      Wokegon         OK     23,657    20          1,495.55
29.911
000005      Kernstin        IL     45,793    20            900.25
18.005
000006      Castigoga       MI     55,831    20          4,260.00
85.200
000007      Gottime         GA      9,321    30          7,542.00
150.840
****** ********  End of report  ********

 F3=Exit      F12=Cancel     F19=Left      F20=Right      F21=Split
```

By examining the report in Figure 8-6, you can see that each of the records in the report contains a BALOWE field that is greater than $400.00. This query sure looks like it performed properly.

☐ Hint: You can and should duplicate this query (and the other queries in this book) on your own machine and run it against the supplied VENDORP file records to assure that you've got it right!

Getting Back

After looking at the Query report, to return to where you were, you just press the ENTER key. If you pressed F5 from the Select Records panel, that is where you will return. If you pressed F5, from the

Define the Query panel, that is where you will return. You can press F5 from just about any place within the Query menus.

If you return to the Select Records panel, just hit ENTER one more time and you will get a Define the Query panel as shown in the panel in Figure 8-7. The selection criteria for the VENDORP case study has been completed.

Figure 8-7 Define The Query - Select Records Completed

```
                        Define the Query
 Query . . . . . . :    FIRSTQ        Option . . . . . :    CREATE
 Library . . . . :     HELLO         CCSID . . . . . . :    37
 Type options, press Enter.  Press F21 to select all.
   1=Select

 Opt    Query Definition Option
      > Specify file selections
      > Define result fields
      > Select and sequence fields
      > Select records
        Select sort fields
        Select collating sequence
        Specify report column formatting
        Select report summary functions
        Define report breaks
        Select output type and output form
        Specify processing options


  F3=Exit          F5=Report          F12=Cancel
  F13=Layout       F18=Files          F21=Select all
```

Selections Completed

As you can see in Figure 8-7, Query/400 has marked the option with a completed sign (">"), which tells you that you have worked this option, and it may be complete. As with all options, after they have the greater than sign, you can still open them up and change them. Don't worry! Query/400 does not count how many times you have altered an option line.

From here, the next item on the agenda for the case study is to go to the Select Sort Fields option, which is covered in Chapter 9. Before you take that journey, however, there are lots more examples you need to examine to help give you the confidence that you can tackle any record selection task.

Sample Selections and Rules

Let's look at a few other examples and a few more rules. Here is the first one:

AGE   LT   21

This is a simple comparison test in which a numeric value of 21 is used. Records in this example are selected only if the AGE field contains a value less than 21.

Some More Rules

It helps to know the rules. But, if you are concerned that some more rules and some more selection examples are going to bog you down right now, move on quickly to Chapter 9 and come back after you have gone through all the options on the Define the Query menu at Chapter 20.

When performing selections, you will notice that most selection tests require just a single value. This value can be either a constant, or a field name. The RANGE test requires two values, which can be either two fields, two constants, or a field and a constant. The LIST and NLIST tests require at least two constant values. The LIKE and NLIKE tests require one value, which is a test pattern.

Don't Make Things Up!

Many of the rules are just common sense. For example, if you use a field name as the value, it must be one of the names in the list in the bottom half of the display. You can't just make it up. Additionally, the type of data in the field (character or numeric) must match the data in the field that you are testing.

Running Out of Typing Room?

Suppose you must type a value that is longer than the amount of space provided by one line. What do you do? There's gotta be a rule for that! Again, it's logical. Finish the line on which you are working and continue on the next line. However, do not type anything in the AND/OR field, or Test fields on the extra lines.

The ability to continue lines comes in handy when you are supplying a range of values. For example, you can place all values for a LIST or RANGE test on one line if they fit OK, or you can list them, up and down, on separate lines.

List of Values

If you are specifying a list of values in the values area, remember to leave a space between the values. You must use one or more blanks to separate your values when you have more than one value in a comparison test. It gets tricky if you have a test value at the very end of a line and you want to continue with more values on the next line. You still must supply a space. Therefore, you must leave a blank in front of the first value on the very next line. This gives you the blank space that you need.

If you forget to leave the blank, Query reads the value on the first line and that on the second as one value, instead of two. In other words, it concatenates the lines even though this is not what you mean. It knows no better when you break the rules. So, the moral is, remember the blanks!

More Sample Selections

Examples of comparison tests using different types of values are:

Field Names:

AND/OR	Field	Test Value
CUSTOMER	EQ	CUSTNAME
DATEB	EQ	DATEBIRTH
COST	LE	PRICE

Numeric Constants:

AND/OR	Field	Test Value
NUMFLD	EQ	75
DAY	RANGE	10 21

SBCS Character Constants:

AND/OR	Field	Test Value
NAME	EQ	'Pete'
STORE	LIST	'DALLAS'
		'CHICAGO'
		'LONDON'
	NLIST	'TEXAS'
		'ILLINOIS'

Date Constant:

AND/OR	Field	Test Value
DTE1	EQ	'2001 01 30'

Time Constant:

AND/OR	Field	Test Value
TIME	LT	'12:30:00'

Timestamp constant:

AO Field	Test Value
TSTMP	GE '1991 01 02 18.00.00'

Pattern values:

Pattern Example 1

AND/OR	Field	Test Value
MNME	LIKE	'J__n'

... such as (John, Jean, Joan, ...)

This entry selects records whenever a "J" is the first letter and an "n" is the fourth letter.

Pattern Example 2

AND/OR   Field   Test Value
LNME   LIKE   '%son%'
...such as
(Stephenson, McPherson, JOHNSON as well
as SONNEYMONN ...)

This entry selects records containing the letters "SON."

Pattern Example 3

AND/OR   Field   Test Value
NAME   LIKE   ' A%'
...(WASHINGTON and JACKSON, but not
ADAMS)

This entry selects records where an "A" is the second letter.

Facts about Query Selections

Up to 100 tests can be used for selection. You can, therefore, make up to 100 comparisons. Each comparison can use as many lines (up to 30 characters per line) as needed, up to a maximum of 100 lines total for all comparisons. Your queries can get pretty big.

The Select Records display (Figure 8-1) provides six input lines at a time for you to enter comparisons. If you need more than this, use the page down key to get more blank input lines. You can also use the page key to view all of the comparisons that you have entered when you are finished or even when you are in process.

Okay, now who's sick of hitting F5 and getting their data in mish-mash sequence? It's time for Chapter 9, starring the SORT facility in Query. LETS GO SORT.

Chapter 9   Select Sort Fields

Sort: The Next Logical Step

When you have finished all of your selection operations, just keep
pressing ENTER until you return to the main Query/400 panel,
which we know as the Define the Query panel. When you get there,
move down one more line from Record Selection, to the SORT
Specification, as shown in Figure 9-1.

Figure 9-1 Define The Query - Sort

```
                         Define the Query
  Query . . . . . . :    FIRSTQ          Option . . . . . :    CREATE
  Library . . . . :      HELLO           CCSID . . . . . . :     37
  Type options, press Enter.  Press F21 to select all.
    1=Select

  Opt    Query Definition Option
     >   Specify file selections
     >   Define result fields
     >   Select and sequence fields
     >   Select records
    1      Select sort fields
           Select collating sequence
           Specify report column formatting
           Select report summary functions
           Define report breaks
           Select output type and output form
           Specify processing options


   F3=Exit          F5=Report         F12=Cancel
   F13=Layout       F18=Files         F21=Select all
```

To Select Sort fields, take the next option on the panel by placing a
"1" in front of the option, and pressing the ENTER key. You will be
taken to the Select Sort Fields panel, as shown in Figure 9-2.

Figure 9-2 Selecting Sort Fields Panel

```
                         Select Sort Fields

Type sort priority (0 999) and A (Ascending) or D (Descending) for
  the names of up to 32 fields, press Enter.

Sort
Prty A/D Field          Text                              Len  Dec
___   _  VNDNBR         VENDOR NUMBER                       5    0
         NAME           NAME                               25
___   _  ADDR1          ADDRESS LINE 1                     25
         CITY           CITY                               15
___   _  STATE          STATE                               2
___   _  ZIPCD          ZIP'CODE                            5    0
         VNDCLS         VENDOR CLASS                        2    0
         BALOWE         BALANCE OWED                        9    2
___   _  PENLTY         BALOWE*.02                          7    3
                                                             Bottom
   F3=Exit        F5=Report       F11=Display text    F12=Cancel
F13=Layout       F18=Files        F20=Renumber        F24=More keys
```

Defining the Sort Criteria

As you can see in the panel in 9-2, all of the fields we selected for the query are available, including the calculated field, PENLTY. Let's sort this file in ascending order by STATE. In this way, you can see all of the records, segregated by state. Within each state, let's sort in descending sequence by the PENLTY field so you can see the biggest penalty payer in each state at the top of the list for that state. And, just in case we have a few identical penalty amounts, let's sort these within CITY.

Defining the Sort Fields

In computer terms, we might say that the major sort field is STATE, the intermediate sort field is PENLTY (descending) and the minor sort field is CITY. We might also say it a different way. This sort will be on CITY, within PENLTY (descending), within STATE.

The way Query/400 likes to refer to the notion of major, intermediate sorting, and minor total is with a sort priority value. Up to 9 priorities can be specified, giving nine levels of sorting. That's lots more than just major, intermediate, and minor. The lower the number, the higher the priority. Therefore, for our example, we would have a sort level breakdown of priority 3, within priority 2, within priority 1.

Coding the Sort Panel

Let's take this new knowledge to the Select Sort Fields panel in Figure 9-3, and put in the coding necessary to get the job done.

Figure 9-3 Selecting Your Sort Fields

```
                        Select Sort Fields

   Type sort priority (0 999) and A (Ascending) or D (Descending) for
     the names of up to 32 fields, press Enter.

   Sort
   Prty A/D Field           Text                          Len  Dec
    __   _   VNDNBR          VENDOR NUMBER                   5   0
             NAME            NAME                           25
    __   _   ADDR1           ADDRESS LINE 1                 25
    3    A   CITY            CITY                           15
    1_   _   STATE           STATE                           2
    __   _   ZIPCD           ZIP'CODE                        5   0
             VNDCLS          VENDOR CLASS                    2   0
             BALOWE          BALANCE OWED                    9   2
    2    D   PENLTY          BALOWE*.02                      7   3
                                                        Bottom
   F3=Exit          F5=Report        F11=Display text   F12=Cancel
   F13=Layout       F18=Files        F20=Renumber       F24=More keys
```

Sort Priority

In Figure 9-3, you specify the sequence for sorting by placing the priority number next to the field that you select.

Ascending / Descending Order

You also specify whether the field should be sorted in ascending or descending sequence (A/D). If you specify nothing in the A/D field, Query/400 defaults the field to ascending sequence.

Again, from our discussion above, we know that the lower the number chosen, the more major the field is in the sort. You can choose up to 32 fields for your sorting. In the example in Figure 9-3, we have chosen to sort on the STATE, PENLTY (descending) and CITY. This will give us a handy reference report by state.

After you press the ENTER key after you select your sort fields, you will see the panel change as in Figure 9-4.

Figure 9-4 Selecting Your Sort Fields

```
                         Select Sort Fields

  Type sort priority (0 999) and A (Ascending) or D (Descending) for
    the names of up to 32 fields, press Enter.

  Sort
  Prty A/D Field         Text                              Len  Dec
  1_    A  STATE         STATE                             2
  2     D  PENLTY        BALOWE*.02                        7    3
  3     A  CITY          CITY                              15
  __    _  VNDNBR        VENDOR NUMBER                     5    0
           NAME          NAME                              25
  __    _  ADDR1         ADDRESS LINE 1                    25
  __    _  ZIPCD         ZIP CODE                          5    0
           VNDCLS        VENDOR CLASS                      2    0
           BALOWE        BALANCE OWED                      9    2

                                                          Bottom
  F3=Exit         F5=Report       F11=Display text   F12=Cancel
  F13=Layout      F18=Files       F20=Renumber       F24=More keys
```

Finishing Up the Sort

You can see that Query/400 brings the sort fields right to the top and it places the "A," for ascending, in all fields, such as STATE, where it was not specifically designated. Now, you may want to see how this all looks. Press F5, and you will get a quick query report to the screen. Then, press F20 once so that you can see the STATE, CITY, and PENLTY fields, as in Figure 9-5.

Figure 9-5 F5 Quick Query Report with Sort

```
                         Display Report
                                    Report width . . . . . :      130
  Position to line  . . . . .          Shift to column . . . . . .
  Line    .6....+....7....+....8....+....9...+...10....+...11....+...12....+...13
             CITY          STATE  ZIP CODE  VENDOR    BALANCE    LATE
                                            CLASS     OWED       PAYMENT
                                                                 PENALTY
  000001    Gottime        GA      9,321    30        7,542.00   150.840
  000002    Chicago        IL     45,903    10        7,500.00   150.000
  000003    Kernstin       IL     45,793    20          900.25    18.005
  000004    Castigoga      MI     55,831    20        4,260.00    85.200
  000005    Wokegon        OK     23,657    20        1,495.55    29.911
  000006    SCRANTON       PA     18,504    20        3,500.00    70.000
  000007    SCRANTON       PA     18,503    30          500.00    10.000
  ****** ********  End of report  ********

  Bottom
  F3=Exit       F12=Cancel      F19=Left      F20=Right      F21=Split
```

The Sort Worked

When you look at the report in Figure 9-5, you can see that the fields are sorted in PENLTY (descending) within STATE, but since there are no duplicate penalty amount records in the states, the CITY sort field is not used. It doesn't hurt for it to remain in the report, however. If more records are added to the file, or if values change in the future, the CITY field sort may have its sort effect.

Moving On

Now that you have selected sort fields and you have run a sample query, you can go back to the Define the Query panel to set up for the next option on the menu. From the display in Figure 9-5, hit the ENTER key until you return to the Define the Query panel, as shown in Figure 9-6.

Figure 9-6 Define The Query - Sort Completed

```
                         Define the Query
  Query . . . . . . :   FIRSTQ         Option . . . . . :   CREATE
  Library . . . . :     HELLO          CCSID . . . . . . :     37
  Type options, press Enter.  Press F21 to select all.
    1=Select

  Opt    Query Definition Option
      >  Specify file selections
      >  Define result fields
      >  Select and sequence fields
      >  Select records
      >  Select sort fields
         Select collating sequence
         Specify report column formatting
         Select report summary functions
         Define report breaks
         Select output type and output form
         Specify processing options

  F3=Exit          F5=Report        F12=Cancel
  F13=Layout       F18=Files        F21=Select all
```

As you can see in Figure 9-6, Query/400 has marked the option with a completed sign (">") which tells you that you have worked this option, and it may be complete.

Now, let's go to Chapter 10 to see how the collating sequence comes into play in the Query game.

Chapter 10   Select Collating Sequence

What's Next?

The question of "What's Next?" is almost always answered in this QuikCourse by the words "Define the Query panel." After every option you define, you want to go back to the Define the Query panel to do the next menu option. Moving down the list from Select Sort Fields in Figure 9-6, you quickly arrive at Select Collating Sequence, as in Figure 10-1.

Figure 10-1 Define The Query - Collating Sequence

```
                          Define the Query
  Query . . . . . . :    FIRSTQ        Option . . . . . :    CREATE
  Library . . . . :    HELLO           CCSID . . . . . . :    37
  Type options, press Enter.   Press F21 to select all.
     1=Select

  Opt    Query Definition Option
         >  Specify file selections
         >  Define result fields
         >  Select and sequence fields
         >  Select records
         >  Select sort fields
     1      Select collating sequence
            Specify report column formatting
            Select report summary functions
            Define report breaks
            Select output type and output form
            Specify processing options

   F3=Exit           F5=Report         F12=Cancel
   F13=Layout        F18=Files         F21=Select all
```

Because this is not a well-known topic, we devote a few extra paragraphs so that we can all be in synch. If things don't always seem to come together the way you conceive your query, it may be that your default collating sequence is not doing the trick for you. For instances such as these, Query/400 using the Select Collating Sequence option, as shown in Figure 10-1. This provides several standard alternate collating sequences, as well as the ability for you to build your own alternate collating sequence. In this way, you may be able to precisely control how collating (sorting) and comparisons are performed for your queries.

Press ENTER, after filling in the panel, as in Figure 10-1.

What is a Collating Sequence?

Quite simply, the collating sequence is the relative value of one character (A, B, C, %, @, 1, 2, 3) to another. It is what decides that an "A" should sort before a "1" on a report, or a "#" before an "*." You might envision a table with every graphic character that you might see on the face of your keyboard positioned on the left side. On the right side, you would see a numeric value from 0, to 255 that assigns a numeric collating value to the character. For the table to make an "A" less than a "1" for example, the A's right side value would have to be a lower number than the number 1. Thus, a big "A" might have a collating value of 100, a small "a" might be 150 and the number "1" might be 200.

Default Collating Sequences

Every machine has a default collating sequence, and the AS/400 actually has many. Collating sequences have been around for a long time. For example, one of the first IBM collating sequences was called Hollerith code, named after Herman Hollerith, the inventor of the punched card. Later, an internal code was created by IBM. It defined 64 characters, and was called BCD, meaning binary coded decimal.

IBM Extends the Code

When IBM changed the basic storage unit to what is known as a byte in computereeze, the byte was capable of up to 256 different characters, so IBM defined a new code called EBCDIC. You can see BCD within this. As you might expect, it was the extension of BCD. Instead of EBCD, for Extended Binary Coded Decimal however, it was dubbed EBCDIC for Extended Binary Coded Decimal Interchange Code.

Non IBM Manufacturers Did Not Agree

Of course, as non-IBM computer manufacturers developed their own byte-based hardware systems, they did not agree that IBM should define the collating values for all of the characters. They got together and defined their own coding structure. They called theirs ASCII. This stands for the American Standard Code for Information Interchange. It almost sounds like it would be un-American to not use ASCII. As history unfolded, it was us against them, as IBM used EBCDIC, and everybody else in the industry used ASCII.

Intel Chose ASCII

When IBM announced its PC back in 1980, it chose the Intel 8088 processor as the basis for the system. The Intel chip was not an IBM offering, so it naturally used the ASCII coding structure. Thus, for a midrange or mainframe IBM system to "talk" to a PC, one or the other machines had to convert the codes to the proper collating sequence.

Country Coding

As personal computers became more and more the norm, rather than the exception, other countries were not fully pleased with EBCDIC or ASCII, and needed substitutions, such as the comma for the period, and the "#" for a "$" sign in British currency. IBM responded with the notion of the CCSID (Coded character set ID). Unfortunately, many industry players, including Microsoft, balked at the idea, and continued to do their own thing

What is a CCSID?

CCSIDs have a number from 0, to 65535, giving 65,536 different potential collating sequences. ASCII and EBCDIC continue to exist, with each having various CCSIDs. IBM's intent was to satisfy the requirement for multilingual computers. For example, the code for US English is 037 and for Britain the CCSID is 285.

That's more than enough on CCSIDs for us. Developers hate CCSIDs, and yet they love them. They are tough to remember and to fully understand, yet CCSIDs can make things easier in a cross system and cross continent network.

Your Own CCSID

When you create an alternate collating sequence so that, for example, a "b" sorts before an "a," you are, in essence, creating your own temporary CCSID. Even though you can, doesn't mean you should. There should be little reason for most users to ever create their own CCSID or mess with alternate collating sequences. Thus, the collating sequence probably will remain one of the unchecked menu options as you do your own queries.

The Query/400 collating sequence is used for character fields when sorting, selecting records, joining files, finding minimum and maximum values, and determining when a control break has occurred. For most of us, the default is fine. If you choose to specify an alternate sequence, there is some additional control you can take in how it is used in comparisons. This is covered with the eleventh and last option from the Define the Query panel.

Practice Changing Collating Sequence

For you to change the collating sequence for a particular query, take the option as in Figure 10-1, and press ENTER. You will be taken to the panel as shown in Figure 10-2.

Figure 10-2 Selecting an Alternate Collating Sequence

```
                    Select Collating Sequence

The selected collating sequence will be used for character fields when
sorting, selecting records, joining files, finding minimum and maximum
values, and determining when a control break has occurred.


Type choices, press Enter.

   Collating sequence
      option . . . . . . .   1              1=Hexadecimal
                                            2=Query for AS/400 English
                                            3=Define the sequence
                                            4=Translation table
                                            5=System sort sequence

   For choice 4=Translation table:
      Table  . . . . . . .                  Name, F4 for list
         Library  . . . . .                 Name, *LIBL, F4 for list


 F3=Exit          F4=Prompt         F5=Report    F10=Process/previous
 F12=Cancel       F13=Layout        F17=Job sequence    F24=More keys
```

The Hexadecimal Default

The Query/400 default, and the selection most people make by
default, is to use the hexadecimal collating sequence (option 1),
which is really the EBCDIC collating sequence. The EBCDIC
(Extended Binary Coded Decimal Interchange Code) sequence sorts
some special characters (#, etc.) between letters. EBCDIC collating
sequence puts lower case letters before upper case letters in the
sequence (a z, A Z). Thus, a lower case "b" would collate before an
upper case "A."

National Language Collating

Option 2, for English-based systems, is the English collating
sequence. This option is tuned to the national language support on
your machine. Thus if you are using German as your national
language, your collating sequence would reflect German when you
use option 2. Using the English sequence, character data is sorted in
a different order than when using the EBCDIC sequence. As an
example, fields with "a" and "A" are sorted together because both
characters have the same sequence number in the English collating
sequence.

Define Your Own

If you pick option 3, the Define Collating Sequence display pops up. This assumes that you want to define your own collating sequence to be used with a specific query or for all the queries that you create. The collating sequence indicates the order that all the characters in character fields are to be arranged or operated on. The panel in Figure 10-3 shows how easy it would be, using option 3, to define your own collating sequence to the AS/400 for this query's purpose. If you select option 3, this is what you see :

Figure 10-3 Defining Your Own Alternate Collating Sequence

```
                        Define Collating Sequence

   CCSID . . . . . . . . . . . . . :        37

   Position to . . . . . . . . . .          Char

   Type sequence number (0 9999) for each character, press Enter.
     (Use the same sequence number to have characters collate in a group.)

   Sequence  Char    Sequence  Char    Sequence  Char    Sequence  Char
      10                90       c        140      h        190      M
      20       □        90       C        140      H        190      m
      30       □       100       d        150      i        200      N
      40               100       D        150      I        200      n
      50       '       110       e        160      J        210      O
      60       _       110       E        160      j        210      o
      70       a       120       f        170      K        220      P
      70       A       120       F        170      k        220      p
      80       b       130       g        180      L        230      Q
      80       B       130       G        180      l        230      q
                                                        More...   F3=Exit
   F11=Hex chars     F12=Cancel  F14=Hexadecimal F15=Language seq.   F16=Use
   default   F17=Job sequence   F24=More keys   Collating sequence initialized
   from national language sequence.
```

As you can see in Figure 10-3, by rolling (more) you can get even more characters to alter. Also, the default on this panel is the national language sequence, which in our case is English, so if you want to change it, make sure you get it right, or it will really make your reports look strange.

To change the collating sequence of an "A," for example, change it from 70, to wherever you want it to sort, say 85, and press ENTER. The effect of this change would be to have B's sorting before A's. It might look a little funny on your reports so, on second thought, let's not do it.

If you think of a different value to place your "A," you may have to roll a few times to find a good place for it. In reality, it is pretty good the way it is, and unless you must, do not change your collating sequence.

Period.

We recommend no changes to the collating sequence, and there are none made in the VENDORP case study. After you have made your changes, if any – hopefully none, after taking option 3, press ENTER until you get back to the Define the Query panel, as in Figure 10-4.

Figure 10-4 Define The Query - Collating Sequence

```
                        Define the Query
  Query . . . . . . :    FIRSTQ         Option . . . . . :    CREATE
  Library . . . . :      HELLO          CCSID . . . . . . :    37
  Type options, press Enter.  Press F21 to select all.
    1=Select

  Opt    Query Definition Option
       > Specify file selections
       > Define result fields
       > Select and sequence fields
       > Select records
       > Select sort fields
       > Select collating sequence
         Specify report column formatting
         Select report summary functions
         Define report breaks
         Select output type and output form
         Specify processing options

   F3=Exit           F5=Report         F12=Cancel
   F13=Layout        F18=Files         F21=Select all
```

As you can see in Figure 10-4, Query/400 has marked the option with a completed sign (">") which tells you that you have worked this option, and it may be complete.

Now, let's go to Chapter 11 to see how we can use the Report Column Formatting option to our advantage.

Chapter 11   Specify Report Column Formatting

Getting Reports Gussied Up!

After you have your collating sequence worked out, it's time to go back to the Define the Query menu panel again and move on down the list. The next stop after collating sequence is Specify Report Column Formatting, as shown in Figure 11-1.

Figure 11-1 Define The Query - Report Column Formatting

```
                        Define the Query
 Query . . . . . . :   FIRSTQ          Option . . . . . :   CREATE
 Library . . . . :    HELLO          CCSID . . . . . . :      37
 Type options, press Enter.  Press F21 to select all.
   1=Select

 Opt    Query Definition Option
       > Specify file selections
       > Define result fields
       > Select and sequence fields
       > Select records
       > Select sort fields
       > Select collating sequence
    1    Specify report column formatting
         Select report summary functions
         Define report breaks
         Select output type and output form
         Specify processing options

 F3=Exit         F5=Report        F12=Cancel
 F13=Layout      F18=Files        F21=Select all
```

When you place a "1" next to the Specify Report Column Formatting option and press ENTER, you get the first Specify Report Column Formatting panel as shown in Figure 11-2.

Figure 11-2 Report Column Formatting

```
                  Specify Report Column Formatting
```

```
Type information, press Enter.
  Column headings:  *NONE, aligned text lines

                  Column
Field             Spacing        Column Headings          Len  Dec   Edit
VNDNBR              0            Vendor                    __5  _0
                                 Number
                                 _____
NAME                2            Vendor                    _25   __
                                 Name
                                 _____
BALOWE              2            Address Line 1            _25  _2

                                 _____
                                                            More...
F3=Exit        F5=Report     F10=Process/previous   F12=Cancel
F13=Layout     F16=Edit      F18=Files              F23=Long comment
```

Defaults First

The default for column formatting for this VENDORP case study is
shown in Figure 11-2. The definitions are taken from the database,
as created by the programmer / analyst. The column heading values
are superimposed upon the Query/400 definition as a starter set.
With this screen, you get your opportunity to change these values.

Why Change The Report Defaults?

You might ask, "Why would you want to change these defaults as
assigned by programmers and analysts in the database?"

Here are a few reasons:

1.   The change is just for this query, so it is okay!

2.   The database may have no column headings.

3.   The column headings may be poor choices.

4.   The column headings may be too long for the field, causing fields to not fit.

5.   The default spacing may cause fields not to fit.

6.   Certain field lengths, as used in this query, may cause fields not to fit.

Making Format Definitions Better

What can you do generically to make your definitions better?

1.   Change the formatting of your report from the above screen.

2.   Adjust column headings, spacing, and editing of numeric fields.

What Can You Do Specifically?

1.   Make the prompts narrower in width.

2.   Use more lines for your prompts to help make them narrower.

3.   Assure that prompts are no wider than the field length.

4.   Try field spacing at zero to see if your report is readable.

5.   Redefine as smaller, fields which 99.9% of the time
        contain smaller values.

Editing

Besides making things fit, your objective may be to make things make
more sense. For example, if the database does not have an edit code
for numeric values such as large dollar amounts and dates, you can
use editing in Query to have the fields properly formatted.

The last column in Figure I-11 is for a mark to say that a field has
been edited. Pressing F16 on this panel gives you a panel which
permits you to change how fields are edited. You can use this to take
the commas out of dates and put commas into dollar values. You can
permit negative values to appear with CR signs or minus signs while
either taking out leading zeros or assuring that they will print. That's
what editing is all about.

Check How Your Report Looks

As we have been saying all along, but it bears repeating, at any time
while you are designing your queries, you can hit the F5 key to see
how well your report is going to format. Let's see what ours looks
like now by pressing F5. The results are shown in Figure 11-3.

Figure 11-3A   Display Report

```
                          Display Report
                              Repo rt width . . . . . :
135
Position to line  . . . . .              Shift to column  . . . . . .
Line
....+....1....+....2....+....3....+....4....+....5....+....6....+....7..
        VENDOR   VENDOR                    ADDRESS LINE 1           CITY
        NUMBER   NAME

000001    10    Thinking Clocks          43 Timestamp Rd        Gottime
000002    25    A MACHINE CORP.          1345 Prill Avenue      Chicago
000003    30    D CONTROLS               45 Fognetta Place
Kernstin
000004    56    Feenala Grund Mfg.       765 Neophite Blvd
Castigoga
000005    26    B MACHINERY              45 Ginzo Lane          Wokegon
000006    48    DENTON AND BALL          7934 S SCRANTON AVE
SCRANTON
000007    46    K D BUTTS WALLACE INC    2150 TOUGHY
SCRANTON
****** ********  End of report  ********

                                                               Bottom
F3=Exit       F12=Cancel      F19=Left     F20=Right      F21=Split
First column of report.
```

Display Your Reports

We did not exit Query to get the report in Figure 11-3A. As noted previously, the results of your queries can be viewed incrementally as you build all of the specifications, one menu definition at a time. Many query builders use F5 to assure that the query is doing the job as they progress through all of the steps. By the time they have completed all of the steps, they know the query will work as intended. With F5, there is no need to wait until the end to see what it will look like.

Windowing/Splitting Records

As you look at reports that have not been built to fit on one screen panel, such as the one in Figure 11-3A above, you naturally want to see the rest of the report. We have discussed Query/400's windowing facility so that you can shift a report to the left or right and view portions of the report through the display panel "window." As you know, you can press F20 to "window right" as we have been doing to see the BALOWE and PENLTY fields in the report. Sometimes, when there is a lot of spacing, or a lot of fields, it can take a lot of F20s to get to the specific field you want to view.

Of course, as we learned, if you want to get back to the front part of the report, after you have windowed, you can window the report in the other direction by pressing F19. So, F20 scrolls right, and F19 scrolls left.

Split Screen

Query/400 also has a nice split screen option (F21) which we have not shown until now. This is very handy if you want to hold record identifying information, such as a customer number or name on the left hand side of the screen while you scroll the information on the right. For example, you might position your cursor at column 21 and hit F21. Then, as you can see in Figure 11-3B, columns 22 through 80 would scroll and columns 1 through 21 would remain fixed on the left side.

Figure 11-3B Split Screen - Poorly Edited Zip Code

```
                          Display Report
                                  Report width . . . . . :
 135
  Position to line  . . . . .          Shift to column  . . . . . .
  Line    ....+....1....+....2. |
 7....+....8....+....9....+...10....+...11....+..
           VENDORVENDOR       |     STATE  ZIP CODE  VENDOR
 BALANC
           NUMBERNAME         |                      CLASS
 OWED
                              |
  000001  00010Thinking Clocks |      GA     9,321    30
 7,542.0
  000002  00025A MACHINE CORP. |      IL    45,903    10
 7,500.0
  000003  00030D CONTROLS      |      IL    45,793    20
 900.2
  000004  00056Feenala Grund M |      MI    55,831    20
 4,260.0
  000005  00026B MACHINERY     |      OK    23,657    20
 1,495.5
  000006  00048DENTON AND BALL |      PA    18,504    20
 3,500.0
  000007  00046K D BUTTS WALLA |      PA    18,503    30
 500.0

  F3=Exit      F12=Cancel      F19=Left      F20=Right      F21=No split
```

This certainly helps in understanding to which records the scrolled values pertain. This is similar to function available in spreadsheet programs such as Quattro Pro and Excel.

Editing Zip Code, Etc.

When we were back at panel 9-5, and again in Figure 11-3B, you may have noticed that the zip code field is edited as if it is a dollar value. It has a comma separator using the default edit code of Query/400, which suppresses leading zeros, and adds comma separators and decimals. This "J" edit code also adds a minus sign if the value is negative.

Zip code does not need such editing. There is another edit code (X) which you can use instead of the "J." It does no editing. Thus, you can see the leading zeroes in the ZIP, and there will be no commas.

Check Out VNDNBR

By the way, the Vendor Number field VNDNBR is also a numeric field with a length of 5 and decimals of 0. Are you wondering why it did not suffer the same plight of the ZIPCD field? The answer is that it did. The zeroes were suppressed. However, there is no VNDNBR field larger than two positions, so there were no commas added. There were also no negative vendor numbers to deal with, so there were no numbers edited with minus signs either. It was wrong, but it looked right.

Making the Edit Changes

Okay, enough of checking things out. Let's do something. Let's change the edit codes of both VNDNBR, and ZIPCD to "X," but first, let's change the spacing between Field 1 (VNDNBR) and Field 2 (NAME) to zero, as shown in the panel in Figure 11-4.

Figure 11-4 Report Column Formatting

```
                        Specify Report Column Formatting

  Type information, press Enter.
    Column headings:  *NONE, aligned text lines
```

```
                   Column
Field              Spacing        Column Headings              Len  Dec
Edit
VNDNBR                0           Vendor                       __5  _0
                                  Number
                                  _____

NAME                  0           Vendor                       _25  __
                                  Name
                                  _____

BALOWE                2           Address Line 1               _25  _2

                                  _____
                                                        More...
F3=Exit        F5=Report      F10=Process/previous    F12=Cancel
F13=Layout     F16=Edit       F18=Files               F23=Long comment
```

Compared to how the panel was in Figure 11-2, as you can see in
Figure 11-4, the spacing has been changed from 2, to zero. When
you see the report in Figure 11-8, you will notice that column1 and
column2 of the report on the display are closer than in Figure 11-3A.

Start Editing VNDNBR

To perform editing on a field, you first position the cursor on the field
in the Specify Column Formatting area, and then you press F16 to
add editing. We want to edit the ZIPCD and the VNDNBR fields.
Let's do VNDNBR first since its on the first panel.

From the panel shown in Figure 11-4, position the cursor on the line
with VNDNBR. The cursor can be in any column or any of the three
rows carved out for the VNDNBR field information. When you
press F16 after positioning properly, you will be taken to the Edit
panel, as shown in Figure 11-5.

Figure 11-5 Report Column Formatting

```
                      Define Numeric Field Editing

Field . . . . . . . . :   VNDNBR
Text  . . . . . . . . :   VENDOR NUMBER
Heading 1 . . . . . . :   VENDOR
Heading 2 . . . . . . :   NUMBER
Heading 3 . . . . . . :
Length  . . . . . . . :   5
Decimal . . . . . . . :   0
Sample  . . . . . . . :   99,999

Type choice, press Enter.
   Edit option . . . . .    1      1=Numeric editing choices
                                   2=Date or time editing choice
                                   3=Edit code
                                   4=Edit word

F3=Exit        F5=Report      F10=Process/previous  F11=Change sample
F12=Cancel     F13=Layout     F16=Remove edit          F18= Files
```

There are a number of ways you can change the editing of the
VNDNBR field from this panel. If you leave the Edit option at the
value "1," with which it is primed when you arrive, and you press
ENTER, you get prompted for each and every type of combination
that you can think of for editing. For now, let's look at the Numeric
editing choices that you get with Edit option 1. Press ENTER to
continue from the panel in Figure 11-5.

```
Figure 11-6 Option 1 - Standard Edit Choices
                    Describe Numeric Field Editing
   Field . . . . . . :    VNDNBR
   Type choices, press Enter.

      Decimal point . . . . . . . .   1        1=. 2=, 3=:  4=$ 5=None
      Thousands separator . . . . .   2        1=. 2=, 3='  4=Blank 5=None
      Show negative sign . . . . .    Y        Y=Yes, N=No
        Left negative sign . . . .
        Right negative sign . . . .
      Show currency symbol . . . .    Y        Y=Yes, N=No
        Left currency symbol . . .    $
        Right currency symbol . . .
      Print zero value . . . . . .    Y        Y=Yes, N=No
      Replace leading zeros . . . .   Y        Y=Yes, N=No
        Replace with . . . . . . .    1        1=Blanks
                                               2=Asterisks
                                               3=Floating currency symbol
        Single leading zero . . . .   N        Y=Yes, N=No

   F3=Exit          F5=Report        F10=Process/previous    F12=Cancel
   F13=Layout       F16=Remove edit  F18=Files
```

Dollar Editing Example

As you can see in Figure 11–6, the choices are very understandable.
This may be just the editing ticket for you when you begin to learn
Query/400, because it walks you through all of the options that you
may select. In effect, this is the definition of editing. Just pick and
choose from the menus on the right, and fill in your choices in the
available area.

In spreadsheet terminology, this process is called formatting. You
start with a raw number blob in a database column, such as
638527783. Then, you sprinkle some editing options on it, and voila,
it gets all dressed up and looks like the following number when it hits
your Query report.

$6,385,277.83

Meanwhile, the value inside of the computer does not change. All the commas and accouterments are placed on the numbers at output time only. Internally, the number stays the same. The editing options in Figure 11-6 provide you with the fancy field look, as above.

Date Editing

There are three more Edit options available on the Define Numeric Field Editing menu in Figure 11-5. Let's go back to Figure 11-4, position the cursor again in the VNDNBR line, and hit F16 for editing. Then, from the next panel, shown in Figure 11-5, pick the next option (date editing) by placing a "2" in the editing option field. When you press ENTER, you see the date editing choices, as shown in Figure 11-7.

Figure 11-7 Option 2 - Date Edit Choices

```
                       Describe Date/Time Field Editing
 Field . . . . . . :      VNDNBR

 Type choice, press Enter.
   Date/time separator . . . . .   4    1=.    2=/    3=:    4=    5=,




 F3=Exit          F5=Report          F10=Process/previous      F12=Cancel
 F13=Layout       F16=Remove edit    F18=Files
```

In the Describe Date/Time Field Editing panel, you get to pick the separator character to use for a date or a time field that you would like Query/400 to edit for you. You can see that there are five choices:

period

slash

colon

dash

comma

Query/400 has already selected the dash (option 4) as the separator character for the VNDNBR field. However, you are about to disappoint Query/400, since this is not a date or time field. But now, you know how it's done when you have a date or time field that you want formatted properly. Press ENTER to return to the Specify Report Column Formatting panel, as shown in Figure 11-4.

Using Edit Codes - Option 3

After you have been doing queries for awhile, or you have been programming in RPG with its vast array of edit codes, you may not want to hunt and peck through the possibilities provided you with editing option 1. More than likely, you will use edit codes. With one character, such as a "3," a "J," an "X," or a "Z," you can tell the Query/400 program how to edit a field. This simplistic notation gets habit forming.

VNDNBR Editing

To specify an edit code, place your cursor on the VNDNBR field in Figure 11-4, and press F16 again. You will see the panel, as shown in Figure 11-5. Change your selection to "3" to use an EDIT Code. Press the ENTER key. You will be taken to the panel, as shown in Figure 11-8.

Figure 11-8 Report Column Formatting

```
                        Specify Edit Code

  Field . . . . . . . . :    VNDNBR

  Type choices, press Enter.

    Edit code . . . . . .    J      1 4, A D, J Q, W Z, user defined 5 9

    Optional edit code
      modifier  . . . . .           1=Asterisk fill
                                     2=Floating currency symbol



  F3=Exit        F5=Report       F10=Process/previous    F12=Cancel
  F13=Layout     F16=Remove edit    F18=Files
```

Notice that Query/400 thinks there is "J" edit code already there. We saw the result of this editing in the report. By default, the "J" edit code provides leading zero suppression, decimals, commas, and a minus sign if the field is negative. That's what we had been getting in both the VNDNBR, and ZIPCD fields.

We are about to change that. Before you hit ENTER, change the "J" value above to "X." The "X" edit code says that there is no edit code. In this way, you get rid of decimals, commas, leading zero suppression, and the potential for a minus sign (more room). In this case, you are changing the VNDNBR field. Shortly after this, you will change the ZIPCD field using the same process. After you type the big "X," press the ENTER key.

ZIPCD Editing

You will return again to the Specify Report Column Formatting panel, as shown in Figure 11-4. To change the ZIPCD field, from the panel in 11-4, roll forward until you find the ZIPCD field (last one of three,) as shown in Figure 11-9.

Figure 11-9 Report Column Formatting

```
                    Specify Report Column Formatting

   Type information, press Enter.
     Column headings:  *NONE, aligned text lines

                      Column
   Field              Spacing      Column Headings       Len  Dec  Edit
   CITY                  2         CITY                    15
                                   _____

   STATE                 2         STATE                    2   __
                                   _____

   ZIPCD                 2         ZIP CODE                 5   0
                                   _____
                                                              More...
   F3=Exit       F5=Report      F10=Process/previous   F12=Cancel
   F13=Layout    F16=Edit       F18=Files              F23=Long comment
```

Position to the ZIPCD field in Figure 11-9, and press F16 again. You will then see the panel as shown in Figure 11-10.

Figure 11-10 Report Column Formatting

```
                        Define Numeric Field Editing

Field . . . . . . . . :    ZIPCD
Text  . . . . . . . . :    ZIP'CODE
Heading 1 . . . . . . :    ZIP CODE
Heading 2 . . . . . . :
Heading 3 . . . . . . :
Length  . . . . . . . :    5
Decimal . . . . . . . :    0
Sample  . . . . . . . :    99,999

Type choice, press Enter.

    Edit option . . . . .    3      1=Numeric editing choices
                                    2=Date or time editing choice
                                    3=Edit code
                                    4=Edit word

  F3=Exit         F5=Report    F10=Process/previous  F11=Change sample
  F12=Cancel      F13=Layout   F16=Remove edit       F18=Files
```

From the panel in Figure 11-10, make sure the selection is set to 3 to use an EDIT Code. Then press ENTER. You will see the panel in Figure 11-11.

Figure 11-11 Report Column Formatting

```
                        Specify Edit Code

Field . . . . . . . . :    ZIPCD

Type choices, press Enter.

   Edit code . . . . . .   X     1 4, A D, J Q, W Z, user defined 5 9

   Optional edit code
     modifier  . . . . .          1=Asterisk fill
                                   2=Floating currency symbol

  F3=Exit         F5=Report       F10=Process/previous      F12=Cancel
  F13=Layout      F16=Remove edit  F18=Files
```

Getting Your Edit Asterisk (Star)

Of course, as noted above, the panel in Figure 11-11 will have a "J" edit code when you get here. We show the "X" this time, since that is what you are supposed to type. When you type the "X" edit code, press ENTER. You will return to the Specify Report Column Formatting panel, as shown in Figure 11-9. This time, there will be an asterisk in the Edit column for ZIPCD.   If you roll back one, you can see the VNDNBR field also has its "*" for editing.

Wow! Did that take some work?   We edited two fields, and we changed the spacing between two fields.   If we take F5 now, the report will start out looking like the panel shown in Figure 11-12.

Figure 11-12 Report - Shows Reduced Spacing

```
                         Display Report
                                Report width . . . . . :      127
 Position to line  . . . . .         Shift to column  . . . . . .
 Line
 ....+....1....+....2....+....3....+....4....+....5....+....6....+....7.
      VENDORVENDOR                   ADDRESS LINE 1           CITY
      NUMBERNAME

 000001  00010Thinking Clocks         43 Timestamp Rd         Gottime
 000002  00025A MACHINE CORP.         1345 Prill Avenue       Chicago
 000003  00030D CONTROLS              45 Fognetta Place       Kernstin
 000004  00056Feenala Grund Mfg.      765 Neophite Blvd       Castigoga
 000005  00026B MACHINERY             45 Ginzo Lane           Wokegon
 000006  00048DENTON AND BALL         7934 S SCRANTON AVE     SCRANTON
 000007  00046K D BUTTS WALLACE INC   2150 TOUGHY             SCRANTON
 ******  ********  End of report   ********

                                                            Bottom
  F3=Exit      F12=Cancel      F19=Left      F20=Right      F21=Split
```

Notice what the zero-spacing option bought us between the first two fields.   Okay, maybe we don't really want zero spacing, but you can sure see that the change worked between the VNDNBR field and the NAME field.   Did you notice anything else?   The "X" edit code took away the default zero suppression and placed the zeroes in front of the VNDNBR fields in the report.

Now, let's go see the ZIPCD field.   But first, take the cursor and place it on column 25.   Hit F21 to go into split mode. The stuff on the left of the report will stay as you hunt for the ZIPCD field by hitting the F20 key.   Just one F20 and you find your display looks like that in Figure 11-13.

Figure 11-13 Report - ZIPCD Edit Code Worked

```
                         Display Report
                                Report width . . . . . :      127
 Position to line  . . . . .         Shift to column  . . . . . .
 Line    ....+....1....+....2....  |
 7....+....8....+....9....+...10....+...11....
      VENDORVENDOR               |      STATE  ZIP CODE  VENDOR
 BALANCE
      NUMBERNAME                 |                       CLASS      OWED
```

```
000001   00010Thinking Clocks   |          GA      09321     30
7,542.00
000002   00025A MACHINE CORP.    |          IL      45903     10
7,500.00
000003   00030D CONTROLS         |          IL      45793     20
900.25
000004   00056Feenala Grund Mfg. |          MI      55831     20
4,260.00
000005   00026B MACHINERY        |          OK      23657     20
1,495.55
000006   00048DENTON AND BALL    |          PA      18504     20
3,500.00
000007   00046K D BUTTS WALLACE  |          PA      18503     30
500.00
******  ********  End of report  ********

                                                          Bottom
F3=Exit      F12=Cancel      F19=Left      F20=Right      F21=No split
```

You can see that the split worked quite nicely. If you look at the rule line, you can see that the second half of the screen starts at about position 68, while the first half ends at 25. This is a nice tool which is similar to the freeze facility in a spreadsheet. The field we were hunting for, ZIPCD, is right there at position 85, and it does not have any commas. Moreover, the leading zeros are not suppressed. Our little output tricks have worked!

Edit Word Option 4

There is yet another editing option which can be chosen for special situations. You would use an edit word, or edit mask when and if you cannot find the options available in the other three choices which we have fully covered. We would expect that these times would be few and far between.

If you need to use an edit word, you would press F16 on the field to be edited as in Figure 11-4. You would then select option 4 on the panel in Figure 11-5. From there you would get a panel that provides an area for you to build an edit word. When you get to this panel, go to the menu title Specify Edit Word, and press Help or F1. Follow the instructions in the Help text to build the edit word needed to complete your Query report.

When you are satisfied that the output options are as you would like, hit ENTER until you return to the Define the Query prompt, as shown in Figure 11-14.

Figure 11-14 Define The Query - Report Format Completed

```
                          Define the Query
Query . . . . . . :    FIRSTQ            Option  . . . . . :    CREATE
Library . . . . :      HELLO       CCSID . . . . . . :        37
Type options, press Enter.  Press F21 to select all.
  1=Select

Opt     Query Definition Option
      > Specify file selections
      > Define result fields
      > Select and sequence fields
      > Select records
      > Select sort fields
      > Select collating sequence
      > Specify report column formatting
        Select report summary functions
        Define report breaks
        Select output type and output form
        Specify processing options

 F3=Exit          F5=Report          F12=Cancel
 F13=Layout       F18=Files          F21=Select all
```

As you can see in Figure 11-14, Query/400 has marked the option with a completed sign ("＞"), which tells you that you have worked this option, and it may be complete.

Now, let's go to Chapter 12 to see how we can use the Report Summary Functions to create some special totals.

Chapter 12   Select Report Summary Functions

Take a Summary

Moving down the big list from Figure 12-1, the now famous Define the Query menu, you come to the next line: Select report summary functions. This option comes in very handy when you need to summarize information in report form. This is the panel where you can get it done.

Figure 12–1 Define The Query - Summary Functions

```
                        Define the Query
Query . . . . . . :   FIRSTQ            Option . . . . . :   CREATE
Library . . . . :    HELLO           CCSID . . . . . . :      37
Type options, press Enter.  Press F21 to select all.
  1=Select

Opt    Query Definition Option
       > Specify file selections
       > Define result fields
       > Select and sequence fields
       > Select records
       > Select sort fields
       > Select collating sequence
       > Specify report column formatting
   1     Select report summary functions
         Define report breaks
         Select output type and output form
         Specify processing options


 F3=Exit          F5=Report         F12=Cancel
 F13=Layout       F18=Files         F21=Select all
```

IBM Help Text

To describe the summary functions, we originally thought we could kill two birds with one stone. We are big believers in IBM's Help text and we make sure we give IBM kudos for the fine job they did in making sure we do not need thick manuals to use an "ease-of-use" product. IBM's Help text for Query/400 is nothing short of outstanding. It is so good, in many cases, you really do not need a manual.

To describe the Select report summary functions, therefore, we had intended to show an amalgamation of the wonderful Help text panels in their IBM form. The format was to be a screen panel which would be built by cut and paste and would have more than the normal 24 lines. We never thought that IBM would have used so much Help text about one Query/400 topic. The Figure with all of this text would have been Figure 12-1. We intended to use it to describe the function of the Select report summary functions option,and demonstrate the facility of Query Help text – at the same time.

Help Text for You

To see the Help text for summary functions, you can pick the Select report summary functions option as in Figure 11-14 and press ENTER. This takes you to the Select Report Summary Functions menu, as shown in Figure 12-2. After positioning the cursor to the screen title, press the Help key, or F1. This takes you to the main Help text for the menu. From this first screen, you can roll through all of the Help text for this option.

Capture Help Text

Since our original intention was to include all of this Help text in this chapter, we captured each panel as we rolled through the Help text for the Select Report Summary Functions menu. As we rolled, we pasted each Help text screen shot into a document work area.

Something happened after all the panels had been pasted. We learned just how voluminous the Help text actually is. We were even more impressed with IBM's ability in both quality and quantity to fill this product with such wonderful Help and instructions. However, there was way too much to show you in this Chapter, so we decided to make Figure 12-2 a shadow of its potentially former self.

Summary Help

Now, let's look at the new, slimmer, Help text in Figure 12-2. The text in the panel describes, in fine detail, the functions that can be used when you choose the Select report summary functions option which we are now discussing. The Help text, therefore, can demonstrate the power of IBM's Help text facility, and it can "help" you understand how to get the most from the Select report summary functions option.

Figure 12-2 Summary Functions - Help & How To!

Help   Report Summary Functions Help
   The Select Report Summary Functions display allows you to specify summary functions for fields that you want summary information about.

You can get summary information for any and all fields that are included in your query report. Depending on the type of field, you can specify one or more (or all) of the following types of summary functions for each field in your report: total, average, minimum value, maximum value, and count. All of them can be used for numeric fields, and all except total and average can be used for character, date, time, and timestamp.

For each field that you specify summary functions, Query calculates summary values and includes them in the report. Query calculates these summary values at each report break (break levels 1 through 9) defined in this query and at the end of the report (break level 0).

   Each type of summary is shown on a separate line in the report, with a descriptive abbreviation shown on the left of the summary values.

For example, assume that your query has a numeric result field named   More...

Help   Report Summary Functions Help
ITEMTOT defined using the expression QUANTITY * ITEMCOST
two numeric fields being multiplied together). These two fields are
used to calculate the cost of each item ordered in the ITEM field.
You might define the following summary functions for those fields:
count for the ITEM field, total and maximum for the QUANTITY
field, maximum for the ITEMCOST field, total and maximum for
the ITEMTOT field, and maximum for the DATEPUR field. The
following is an example of how part of a report might look for a
customer named Z Z Smith:

```
ITEM      QUANTITY  ITEMCOST   ITEMTOT    DATE PURCHASED
              Bolt    12         .10       1.20      1991 05 01
              Hammer   2        8.50      17.00      1991 07 11
              Ruler    1        2.00       2.00      1991 09 13
              Screw    6         .05        .30      1991 11 16

          Totals for: Z Z Smith
          TOTAL       21                  20.50
          MAX         12        8.50      17.00      1991 11 16
          COUNT  4

      Summary function results, if defined, can appear in all three types
      (displayed, printed, and database) and both forms (detailed and
      summary) of output, with one exception:  they cannot be included
      if  the report is to a database file in detailed form.

      For more information about selecting and using report summary
      functions, see Chapter 11 of the Query User's Guide.
```

Selecting Summary Functions

As noted above in the Help text discussion, the next step is to take the
Select report summary functions from the Define the Query menu.
After you type a "1" and press ENTER, as in the panel shown in
Figure 11-14, you get a screen aptly titled: Select Report Summary
Functions. This screen is shown in Figure 12-3.

From here, let's add some summary functions to the VENDORP
case study example. Considering that there are only two fields
(BALOWE and PENLTY) which are real candidates for any
summary work (dollar fields), there is little doubt as to which fields to
select. Now, let's move to the panel in Figure 12-3, so that you can
use it to enable your summary definitions.

Figure 12-3 Select Report Summary Functions

```
                     Select Report Summary Functions

Type options, press Enter.
  1=Total    2=Average    3=Minimum    4=Maximum    5=Count

    Options     Field          Text                        Len  Dec

                VNDNBR         VENDOR NUMBER                  5   0
                NAME           NAME                          25
                ADDR1          ADDRESS LINE 1                25
                CITY           CITY                          15
                STATE          STATE                          2
                ZIPCD          ZIP CODE                       5   0
                VNDCLS         VENDOR CLASS                   2   0
  1  2  3  4  5 BALOWE         BALANCE OWED                   9   2
  5  4  3  1  2 PENLTY         BALOWE*.02                     7   3
                                                              Bottom
  F3=Exit       F5=Report    F10=Pro/prev    F11=Display names only
  F12=Cancel    F13=Layout   F18=Files       F23=Long comment
```

Available Functions

On the third line of the panel in Figure 12-3, you can see the
following options:

1=Total
2=Average
3=Minimum
4=Maximum
5=Count

Making the Summary Selections

Since this is an educational exercise, go ahead and select every single
summary function for the BALOWE field and the PENLTY field.
There are five input slots per field. Each field, theoretically, can have
up to five summary functions built against it.

We are changing the theoretical to the practical in this exercise. For
BALOWE and PENLTY to take all summary functions, place a
1,2,3,4, or 5 in any sequence in each of the five slots, as shown at the

bottom of Figure 12-3, preceding the field name. As you can see in the example, the order you specify the functions does not matter. When your panel looks similar to that in Figure 12-3, hit the ENTER key to indicate that you are finished with your summary selections. You will return to the Define the Query panel, as in Figure 11-14.

Quick Summary Report

From the Define the Query menu, hit F5 to get a quick report to see the results. On the first Display Report panel "window," however, you will not find any summary totals. What might be wrong? Actually, nothing is wrong. The panel is not shown because the summary fields are way over on the right side of the report. They are not visible in the first window, so we did not show the panel.

The totals are positioned under the fields (BALOWE and PENLTY) which have been summarized. In order to see these totals, you must window to the right. The F20 key provides this function. When you hit F20, after your first F5, you will then see a window as shown in Figure 12-4. Note that all the summary totals for BALOWE and PENLTY (Total, Average, Minimum, Maximum, and Count) are included on the right side of the window.

Figure 12-4 Summary Total Report - All Summaries Selected

```
                         Display Report
                                Report width . . . . . :      135
  Position to line  . . . . .        Shift to column  . . . . . .
  Line    .+....7....+....8....+....9....+...10....+...11....+...12....+...13....+
          Y            STATE  ZIP CODE  VENDOR          BALANCE       LATE
                                        CLASS            OWED         PAYMENT
                                                                      PENALTY
  000001 time          GA      9,321     30           7,542.00       150.840
  000002 cago          IL     45,903     10           7,500.00       150.000
  000003 nstin         IL     45,793     20             900.25        18.005
  000004 tigoga        MI     55,831     20           4,260.00        85.200
  000005 egon          OK     23,657     20           1,495.55        29.911
  000006 ANTON         PA     18,504     20           3,500.00        70.000
  000007 ANTON         PA     18,503     30             500.00        10.000
  000008
  000009                                FINAL TOTALS
  000010                                TOTAL       25,697.80        513.956
  000011                                AVG          3,671.11         73.422
  000012                                MIN            500.00         10.000
  000013                                MAX          7,542.00        150.840
  000014                                COUNT              7                7
                                                               More...
  F3=Exit     F12=Cancel     F19=Left     F20=Right     F21=Split
  Last column of report.
```

You can see the total, average, minimum, maximum, and count values for both BALOWE and PENLTY in Figure 12-4. These are very powerful Query operations and, as you found out through this QuikCourse chapter, they are very easy to select with Query/400.

Completing the Summary Selections

When you press ENTER, you return to the Define the Query option, as seen in Figure 12-5.

Figure 12-5 Define The Query- Summary Functions Completed

```
                         Define the Query
Query . . . . . . :   FIRSTQ         Option . . . . . :   CREATE
Library . . . . :    HELLO         CCSID . . . . . . :    37
  Type options, press Enter.  Press F21 to select all.
1=Select

Opt    Query Definition Option
     > Specify file selections
     > Define result fields
     > Select and sequence fields
     > Select records
     > Select sort fields
     > Select collating sequence
     > Specify report column formatting
     > Select report summary functions
       Define report breaks
       Select output type and output form
       Specify processing options
  F3=Exit          F5=Report        F12=Cancel
  F13=Layout       F18=Files        F21=Select all
```

As you can see in Figure 12-5, Query/400 has marked the option with a completed sign (">"), which tells you that you have worked this option, and it may be complete.

In this chapter, we used the summary functions to define some final total functions which apply to the whole Query report. Now, let's go to Chapter 13 to see how we can use the Report Break Functions to create some intermediate-level totals for this query definition.

Chapter 13   Define Report Breaks

Breaking Down the Query Report

Moving on down one line using the Define the Query menu panel as
shown in Figure 13-1, from Select report summary functions, we
arrive at our next Query definition opportunity - Define report
breaks.

Figure 13-1 Define The Query- Output Breaks

```
                            Define the Query
  Query . . . . . . :    FIRSTQ          Option . . . . . :    CREATE
  Library . . . . :     HELLO           CCSID . . . . . . :    37
  Type options, press Enter.  Press F21 to select all.
    1=Select

  Opt    Query Definition Option
         > Specify file selections
         > Define result fields
         > Select and sequence fields
         > Select records
         > Select sort fields
         > Select collating sequence
         > Specify report column formatting
         > Select report summary functions
    1      Define report breaks
           Select output type and output form
           Specify processing options

  F3=Exit           F5=Report          F12=Cancel
  F13=Layout        F18=Files          F21=Select all
```

The F5 Quick report in Figure 12-4 shows some nice totals which are
produced only at the end of the run. In essence, they are final totals
representing all of the data processed by this Query report.

How to Code Report Breaks in Query/400

What if you wanted more than summaries at the end of the report?
For example, let's say you want a total for each state. The question

of the day becomes, "How do you code your Query/400 report break to get a total for each state?" We are about to show you.

In the sample data, there are just five states represented in the selection results - Georgia (GA), Illinois (IL), Michigan (MI), Oklahoma (OK), and Pennsylvania (PA).

The Importance of the Sort

You may recall from our Sort definition, that we sorted on STATE as the major field. That is a must in being able to get usable summary totals for each state. It would actually be impossible to get meaningful state totals if we were not sorting on state. This is a point to remember as you are building your Query definitions. You must have the data sequenced at the same levels as the report breaks in order to get reports with intermediate-level totals.

Now, let's go define the STATE field for report breaks by hitting ENTER on the panel, shown in Figure 13-1. This will take you to the panel as shown in Figure 13-2.

Figure 13-2 Defining Report Breaks

```
                         Define Report Breaks

Type break level (1 6) for up to 9 field names, press Enter.
  (Use as many fields as needed for each break level.)

Break     Sort
Level     Prty  Field           Text                      Len   Dec

                VNDNBR          VENDOR NUMBER               5     0
                NAME            NAME                       25
                ADDR1           ADDRESS LINE 1             25
           30   CITY            CITY                       15
  1        10   STATE           STATE                       2
                ZIPCD           ZIP'CODE                    5     0
                VNDCLS          VENDOR CLASS                2     0
                BALOWE          BALANCE OWED                9     2
           20   PENLTY          BALOWE*.02                  7     3
                                                             Bottom
F3=Exit         F5=Report       F10=Proc/prev   F11=Display names only
F12=Cancel      F13=Layout      F18=Files                 F23=Long comment
```

Select from Sort Fields

To set up the definition to break on each state, from the panel in Figure 13-2, type the number "1" next to STATE for a first level total. STATE is noted with a sort level of 10 since, as you may recall, we defined it as the major sort field.

We do not care about CITY or PENLTY in terms of total breaks for this Query report, so there is no reason to define a control level for either of them. You will find, as you do more queries, that sort fields are prime candidates for break fields. Typically, you cannot pick another field and have it work well.

General Information on Report Breaks

Before we wrap up the selection for STATE, let's briefly discuss the capabilities of the report break panel so that you understand how to use this with more complicated queries. In other queries, for example, you may choose to type a number from 1, through 6 in this column for each field that you want defined as a break field. This gives six levels of totals besides the Final Total.

You can also specify multiple break fields for the same break level, as long as you assign no more than nine break fields for all break levels used (max of 6). In other words, at break level 1, you may have, say, three fields. When any one of the three fields changes, from record to record, Query gives the report a break total. So, overall, you can have nine fields selected as break fields as long as some fields share a break level.

Sorted Break Fields

Each defined break field is to be used to cause report breaks. A report break for a particular break level occurs whenever the contents of the break field (or any of the break fields assigned to that level) change from record to record. This would occur in our example as we change from GA, to IL and as we change from IL, to MI etc.

Final Total Break

You get your last break when Query/400 hits the last record of the last group (PA) of records. Since there are no more states, there is a change in the state field from PA, to blank. Moreover, the last record tells the Query program to fire off final totals after the break totals. Whenever a final break is encountered, all intermediate breaks are automatically triggered.

Thus, in the VENDORP case study, you would get a total, after the first change representing Georgia vendors, and then Illinois, etc. But, you would also get a total after the last Pennsylvania record, since there are no more vendors (last record = final totals) in the query. This intermediate total would represent the Pennsylvania vendors.

In addition to the last level total for PA at the end of a report, the definition also calls for a final total. The final total is produced immediately after the group total for the STATE break, as the last set of summary totals for the report. In essence, the same totals which you saw in Figure 12-4 appear at the end of the report — immediately following the last intermediate group total.

Non-sorted Break Fields

Although you can specify any field in the list as a break field (sorted and non-sorted), as a rule, you should use only the sort fields. As you can see, in Figure 13-2, the sort fields have a sort priority number in the next column. Non-sort fields have no sort priority. As a general rule, it is not good to use non-sort fields as break fields, since you may get extra (unwanted) report breaks.

Erroneous Totals

If, for example, you did not sort on STATE, the unsorted data might be arranged in such a way that one record would be for MI, the next for GA, the next for MI, etc. Without a sort on STATE, you would get a separate STATE total for every single record, because of the breaks caused by not sorting.

For the purposes of the VENDORP case study, the report totals would be useless, since the totals would not, in fact, represent the totals for any of the states. Moreover, because the totals would be repeated for each record, the report would be messy and mostly unreadable. If this is an area in which you have particular interest, the IBM Query User's Guide has lots more information about using non-sort fields as break fields. Our general recommendation, however, is, "Don't use them!"

Break Sequence and Sort Priority

Additionally, when you use sort fields as break fields, the break levels should be specified in the same relative order as the sort priority sequence. This makes sense. Otherwise, you force records to compare as breaks, when they really are not breaks, thereby again - just as with non-sort fields, giving extraneous totals.

When assigning break levels, therefore, the highest assignable break level (level 1) should be assigned to a high sort priority number. Break level 2 should be assigned to some lower priority number, and the lowest break level used should be assigned to a low sort priority number.

Back to **VENDORP** Case Study

Now that you have had this little instructional Sort diversion, you can now get ready to resume the VENDORP case study. After you assign the level breaks (1 on STATE in this example), as shown back in Figure 13-2, and you press ENTER, you will get one panel for every break level you have just defined, plus an extra one for the final total. In this case study, you defined just one break. Therefore, you will get two break panels to complete.

On these panels, you get to describe more information about the break totals and the final total. They arrive for you to complete in most significant to least significant total level sequence. Since, in the VENDORP case study, you selected just a final total and one level total, you get the final total panel first, as shown in Figure 13-3. Then, you get the level 1 total panel, as shown in Figure 13-4 for the STATE field.

Figure 13-3 Final Total Report Break

```
                        Format Report Break
Break level  . . . . . . . :   0

Type choices, press Enter.
  (Type &field in text to have break values inserted.)


  Suppress summaries . . . .   N           Y=Yes, N=No

  Break text . . . . . . . .   FINAL TOTALS



Level   Field
  1     STATE

F3=Exit           F5=Report         F10=Process/previous    F12=Cancel
F13=Layout        F18=Files         F23=Long comment
```

Final Total Level

When the FINAL TOTALS break information panel appears, as in Figure 13-3, you may get confused as I did the first few times. You may ask yourself, "Why is the level 1 field, STATE, on this panel?" The answer is that it is there for information purposes only. If you had six total levels defined besides the final total, all six would be listed. On the Final Total panel, you do nothing with the STATE total..

The Million Dollar Summary Question

There is only one question you are asked on this panel. Do you want to suppress summaries? In other words, do you want the totals at this level to be skipped? If you answer, "Yes," skip them. There is no reason to supply a title for the totals. If you answer, "No," then the totals at this level (Final Totals), are printed. Since you have gone this far, however, you might as well print them. Besides, it is a requirement of the VENDORP case study.

Because the panel in Figure 13-3 at this level is for Final Totals, it comes already filled in with the words, "FINAL TOTALS." This is the text which will show by the last total of the report. If you are happy with capital letters and this text, leave it alone, and press ENTER. Otherwise, change the text to your preference, and press the ENTER key. You will be taken to the next most significant level total. In this case study, that is level 1, for STATE, as shown in Figure 13-4.

Figure 13-4 State Field Report Break - Level 1

```
                        Format Report Break

Break level  . . . . . . . :    1

Type choices, press Enter.
  (Type &field in text to have break values inserted.)

  Skip to new page . . . . .    N            Y=Yes, N=No

  Suppress summaries . . . .    N            Y=Yes, N=No

  Break text . . . . . . . .    State Total


Level   Field
  1     STATE

F3=Exit          F5=Report          F10=Process/previous  F12=Cancel
F13=Layout       F18=Files          F23=Long comment
```

State Total Level

First of all, when you arrive at the panel in Figure 13-4, the Break Text field is blank. We have already filled it in for you with an appropriate total title — as you can see. We cleverly used, "State Total," as the break title.

Skip To New Page

There is one additional question in the panel, in Figure 13-4, for level break information vs. final totals. Do you want to skip to a new page? This does not mean, "Do you want the totals on a new page?" It means- after the totals are printed for this break level (STATE in this case study), do you want the next state's information to begin on a clean page, or is it okay to start the next state on the same page as the prior state's totals? Select "N," as shown. This means no new page for the VENDORP Query report.

Suppress Totals

For the second question, just as with FINAL TOTALS, we want the summary totals to print. Therefore, again, do not suppress summaries. There is one more thing different from the FINAL TOTALS panel. For break text, when you get the panel, as noted above, the break text field is blank. Notice that we specified the text for the STATE total.

Get an Intermediate Report

Press ENTER after you have completed the screen to your satisfaction. To get a check as to how the totals look, you may also want to hit the F5 key. If you do so at this time, you would get a report similar to that in Figure 13-5. However, your screen report would not have as many lines.

In order to see the data from the report in 13-5, you would have to roll and press F20 to see the right side of the window. What you are looking at in Figure 13-5, is the last two panels of the report, as sent to the display. It is an amalgamation of the last two screens of the report. You see a little detail from the right side, then the last STATE total, followed by the final total.

Figure 13-5 Report With State and Final Totals - Last Panels

```
                              Display Report
                                    Report width . . . . . :        135
Position to line  . . . . .            Shift to column  . . . . . .
Line
.+....7....+....8....+....9....+...10....+...11....+...12....+...13....+
            Y          STATE  ZIP CODE  VENDOR           BALANCE         LATE
                                        CLASS            OWED
PAYMENT

PENALTY
000027                                  COUNT                  1
1
000028
000029 egon       OK    23,657   20             1,495.55
29.911
000030
000031                                  State Total
000032                                  TOTAL          1,495.55
29.911
000033                                  AVG            1,495.55
29.911
000034                                  MIN            1,495.55
29.911
000035                                  MAX            1,495.55
29.911
000036                                  COUNT                  1
1
000037
000038 ANTON      PA    18,504   20             3,500.00
70.000
000039 ANTON      PA    18,503   30               500.00
10.000
000040
                                                                   More...
000041                                  State Total
000042                                  TOTAL          4,000.00
80.000
000043                                  AVG            2,000.00
40.000
000044                                  MIN              500.00
10.000
000045                                  MAX            3,500.00
70.000
000046                                  COUNT                  2
2
000047
000048                                  FINAL TOTALS
000049                                  TOTAL         25,697.80
513.956
000050                                  AVG            3,671.11
73.422
000051                                  MIN              500.00
10.000
000052                                  MAX            7,542.00
150.840
000053                                  COUNT                  7
7
****** ********  End of report  ********
                                                               Bottom
F3=Exit      F12=Cancel      F19=Left      F20=Right      F21=Split
```

Well, that's about enough for report breaks. You now have summary totals and report breaks built into the VENDORP query case study. By hitting the ENTER key once or twice, you will arrive back at the Define the Query panel as in Figure 13-6.

Figure 13-6 Define The Query- Output Breaks Completed

```
                         Define the Query
Query . . . . . . :    FIRSTQ        Option  . . . . . :    CREATE
Library . . . . :     HELLO         CCSID . . . . . . :      37
Type options, press Enter.  Press F21 to select all.
  1=Select

Opt    Query Definition Option
     > Specify file selections
     > Define result fields
     > Select and sequence fields
     > Select records
     > Select sort fields
     > Select collating sequence
     > Specify report column formatting
     > Select report summary functions
     > Define report breaks
       Select output type and output form
       Specify processing options

 F3=Exit          F5=Report          F12=Cancel
 F13=Layout       F18=Files          F21=Select all
```

As you can see in Figure 13-6, Query/400 has marked the option with a completed sign (">"), which tells you that you have worked this option, and it may be complete.

Now, let's go to Chapter 14 to see the output types and the forms of output we can create with Query/400. After Chapter 14, you may not be satisfied with F5 as your report generator.

Chapter 14   Select Output Type and Output Form

Your Output Is Served!

To get the reports that you have seen shown so far, you have been pressing F5. These all come back to the same display from which you interactively run them. However, you cannot easily show the report on your screen to anybody else. Your PC monitor is too heavy for this to be practical. Thinking of the conundrum you would be in if there were no other option, IBM has rescued Query/400. Built into the magic of Query/400 is a natural way for you to print your report or to send it to a file which can be emailed. But how? ... Not with F5!

You need the next Query/400 option. As you continue your journey down the Define the Query panel, as seen in Figure 14-1, the next line, Select output type and output form, deals with changing the form of your output to a printer or to a database file.

Figure 14-1 Define The Query- Select Output Type & Form

```
                              Define the Query
 Query . . . . . . :    FIRSTQ          Option  . . . . . :    CREATE
 Library . . . . :      HELLO       CCSID . . . . . . :        37
 Type options, press Enter.  Press F21 to select all.
    1=Select


 Opt     Query Definition Option
       > Specify file selections
       > Define result fields
       > Select and sequence fields
       > Select records
       > Select sort fields
       > Select collating sequence
       > Specify report column formatting
       > Select report summary functions
       > Define report breaks
    1    Select output type and output form
         Specify processing options


  F3=Exit           F5=Report          F12=Cancel
  F13=Layout        F18=Files          F21=Select all
```

Direct Your Output

After you pick the option above and you go through the questions in
the sub panels, you'll be able to direct your output the way you want
it. You can run your Query and send your output to a printer, to a
database file, or, if it is already set up to go to one of these, you can
change it back to the display screen — as you choose.

When you select this option from the Define the Query panel by
placing a 1 next to it, and pressing ENTER, you will be taken to the
Select Output Type and Output Form panel as shown in Figure 14-2.

Figure 14-2, Select Output Type and Output Form

```
                    Select Output Type and Output Form

 Type choices, press Enter.

    Output type  . . . . . . . . . .    1      1=Display
                                               2=Printer
                                               3=Database file

    Form of output . . . . . . . . .    1      1=Detail
                                               2=Summary only

    Line wrapping  . . . . . . . . .    N      Y=Yes, N=No
       Wrapping width . . . . . . . .           Blank, 1 378
       Record on one page . . . . . .   N      Y=Yes, N=No

  F3=Exit         F5=Report      F10=Process/previous
  F12=Cancel      F13=Layout     F18=Files
```

And the Options Are

The Select Output Type and Output Form display panel is the vehicle by which you select where you want your query output to go, and in what form you want it to be. You can see the Output type options are (1) display, (2) printer, and (3) database file. The form options are (1) detailed, or (2) summary.

A Few Extra Options

At the bottom of the panel are a few extra options that have to do with how a record is to behave when printed or displayed. For example, you can truncate a record if the whole thing does not fit or you can wrap to the next line. If you are printing large records, with lots of data, such as a real estate property "card," or a personnel record, you can tell the Query program to print just one record per sheet.

Output Type Prompt

By the time you get to this point of the VENDORP case study, you have done all of the difficult technical work for your query. Your query either works, or it doesn't. This panel assumes all of the prior stuff is correct, and it lets you do some schmoozing.

To Print or Not To Print

Of course, it does not force you to schmooze. You can choose not to use this step in defining your query. The default to the display may be all you need. A quick phone call may be what it takes to communicate your query results without hard copy. If you choose to skip this option, the Query/400 report arrives at your workstation as a displayed report in detailed form.

However, you may need hard copy for posterity or for distribution. In this case, you would want to print a paper report. You may also want to give your client or your accountant the report in a database form. In these cases, you have to define the output type and form with this panel and subsequent panels.

The Type Options

From the panel in Figure 14-2, then, to make your output device
selection, you start by typing the number of one of the following type
of output choices to select for your query:

Display
Printer
Database

In the next section of this chapter, we describe how to code the
panels for each of these Type options. After this, we discuss output
form (detail or summary) and line wrapping options.

Three Queries in One?

If a query is built for display, and we run the query, we can certainly
change it to run with a printed report. Likewise, we can again
change it to send the results to a database file. Thus, for each query
definition, we can get at least three types of output reports.

Well, not exactly! When we study the output form prompt, you will
see that for each of the three type options, there are two different
form options. Therefore, the same query can be run six different
ways as follows:

Display   Detail Report
Printer   Detail Report
Database Detail Report
Display   Summary Report
Printer   Summary Report
Database Summary Report

If we add line wrapping options and record on one page options to the VENDORP case study, you can see the combinations increasing to twelve and twenty-four for the same basic query.

Although you can save all twenty-four of these queries under different names for later recall, for the VENDORP project, we have selected one option - the Database Summary option. This serves our purposes since we have yet to work with the database option. Using F5, we have already seen what the detail lines and the summary lines look like on the display. They look very much the same for the printer. The database has not been as explored as much so far in this course.

□ Hint: Though VENDORP is now database- oriented, it would serve you well as you are doing these queries to take as many options of the twenty-for as you can. Observe what happens in each case. Take the printer options, for sure, so you can get a feel for the types of things you might do to make your report look better or to scrunch the columns so that it fits on one page without truncation or wrap.

Examining All the Output Options

We now digress again temporarily, to examine the various options and displays for the three types, the two forms, and the wrapping options. There is a lot of information to cover in this chapter, and mostly, it is not exciting. You can liven up your experience if you copy your query each time on the WRKQRY panel and follow-along to explore the impact of the various options we take in this section. For now, let's examine the Report Type prompt in detail, starting with the Display Output Type.

Display

You can select option 1 from the panel in Figure 14-2, if you want the output of the query to be shown on your display, in detail or summary form. This is very similar to hitting F5. If you happen to run your query in batch, regardless of whether you select option 1, however, the output will not be sent to your display. It will be sent to a printer and not to the display, since a batch job does not have a display device associated with it.

Printer

If you pick option 2, the output of the query is printed on any type of printer, in detailed or summary form. When you select this option, the Define Printer Output display pops up, since the system wants more information about the printout. This is shown in the panel in Figure 14-3 when you press the ENTER key, with option 2 filled-in.

Figure 14-3 Printer Output - Define

```
                    Define Printer Output
Type choices, press Enter.
    Printer  . . . . . . . . .    P1            *PRINT, name
    Form size:
      Length . . . . . . . . .    66            Blank, 1 255
      Width  . . . . . . . . .    132           Blank, 1 378
    Start line . . . . . . . .    3             Blank, 1 255
    End line . . . . . . . . .    63            Blank, 1 255
    Line spacing . . . . . . .    1             1, 2, 3
    Print definition . . . . .    N             Y=Yes, N=No
 F3=Exit          F5=Report      F10=Process/previous
 F12=Cancel       F13=Layout      F18=Files
```

Printer Panels

On the Select output type and output form panel, if you select Printer, you will get each of the panels from Figure 14-3 through 14-6, so that you can better define your printer requirements to the query definition. Unlike the Display option, in which the defaults are typically fine, when you select to print your query, will want to fill in these printer panels to refine your report.

If you are following along on your machine using the COPY query, as we suggest at the beginning of this chapter, feel free to use the defaults for options not yet covered, as you progress through the various panels. You may also choose to take F3 in your lab exercises when you are finished with an option, so that you can save the query, run it, and be prepared to copy the query for the next option.

☐ Note: For instructional purposes, we have opted to complete the printer information and database information within their respective output type sections, rather than first completing all of the Select output type and output form parameters as shown in Figure 14-2. Therefore, in this chapter, you will complete the Output form and Line wrapping sections after you have experienced all of the follow-on panels in the printer and database areas. If you were building a query, you would pick just one output type, whereas we are explaining all three. After picking the output type, say, Printer, you would always complete the Output form and Line Wrapping sections prior to hitting ENTER.

You should use Figures 14-3 to 14-6 to tailor your printed output request. For example, printer spacing and margin information are requested in Figure 14-3. Spooling attributes are added in Figure 14-4. Cover Page information is added in Figure 14-5, and Header and Footer information is added in Figure 14-6.

Define Printer Output

From the Define Printer Output display in Figure 14-3, you can select the specific printer to be used and other characteristics of the printed output. Please note that the panel you are looking at is not set at its defaults. We have already primed the fields with some typical values for a query report. For example, we provided the following:

Printer name   P1. If this report is for your department or another department, providing the proper printer name saves on distribution time.

Form length   66. At six lines per inch of form. On a typical 14 ½ X 11 green bar output form, this equates to 11 inches. When the report is printed on a cut sheet laser printer, 66 lines can print in reduced landscape mode on one 8.5 X 11 sheet of paper.

Form width   132. At ten characters per inch, with an appropriate margin, on a typical 14 ½ X 11 green bar output form, this equates to 13.2 inches plus margin = 14 ½ inches. When the report is printed on a cut sheet laser printer, 132 print positions can print in reduced landscape mode on one 8.5 X 11 sheet of paper.

Start line   3. Of the 66 lines which can be printed, typically the first print line permits some blank space at the top of the form. In this case, two lines are skipped before printing. In conjunction with the End Line parameter, this provides separation between pages.

End line   63. Of the 66 lines which can be printed, typically the last print line permits some blank space at the bottom of the form. In this case, three lines are skipped before hitting form end. In conjunction with the Start Line parameter, this provides separation between pages.

Line spacing   1. You can set the line spacing at 1, 2, or 3, depending on your requirements for the report.

Print definition   N. You have the option of printing the query definition prior to printing the actual query report.

When you are finished typing your attributes in Figure 14-3, hit the ENTER key, and you will be asked more printer questions in Figure 14-4.

Figure 14-4 Printer Output - Define Spooled Output

```
                        Define Spooled Output

Type choices, press Enter.

   Spool the output . . .    Y           Blank, Y=Yes, N=No

   Form type  . . . . . .                Blank, name, *STD

   Copies . . . . . . . .    1           Blank, 1 255

   Hold . . . . . . . . .                Blank, Y=Yes, N=No

F3=Exit          F5=Report          F10=Process/previous
F12=Cancel       F13=Layout         F18=Files
```

Define Spool Output

This panel asks you one major question at the top. Do you want to spool the printed output (like Windows Print Manager,) or do you want to go directly to a printer? Though some choose not to use Spool, with a multi-user system, it is very difficult to assure that a given printer is going to be available at a given moment in time. We plugged in a "Y" for this prompt, since it is good to spool the output, and print it when the printer is available.

Form Type

Most often, you will let the form type default to blank, since you will be printing your reports on whatever paper is in a particular printer.

Number of Copies

If you have a report distribution, you would change the number of copies to equal the number of people who are to receive the report.

Hold the Printout

Finally, you have the option of holding the report. One reason for holding a report would be when you are just creating the query and you would like to assure that it is correct before you print it. You might also hold a query printout so that the intended user can find the report in a particular output queue, and they can decide whether they want to print it or not. They may even choose to move the report to another printer queue.

When you are sure you've got the spooling attributes displayed in Figure 14-4 completed correctly, press ENTER and you will come to the panel in Figure 14-5.

Figure 14-5 Printer Output Specify Cover Page

```
                         Specify Cover Page

  Type choices, press Enter.

    Print cover page . . . . .   Y            Y=Yes, N=No

    Cover page title
  Distribution: Melanie, Bob Cratcett, Scrooge

  F3=Exit          F5=Report          F10=Process/previous
   F12=Cancel       F13=Layout          F18=Files
```

Cover Page

Most users care little about a cover page when they are building their
query. However, the cover page can provide value, especially in the
area of report distribution. Once the Query prints, and the papers sit
with all the other reports in a particular printer tray, it may be
difficult to identify and distribute your report to the proper area.

Many companies use the cover page to specify a distribution. In this
way, there is no guesswork. Before each report is printed, the cover
page serves as its separator from the pack and provides a means of
no-brainer distribution. As you can see, this Query report will be
distributed to Melanie, Bob Cratchet, and Scrooge himself.

The two prompts shown in Figure 14-5 let you build a proper cover
page. When you are finished with these entries, press ENTER and
you will have one more printer options panel to fill out-- Figure 14-6.

Figure 14-6 Printer Output Headings and Footings

```
                   Specify Page Headings and Footings

  Type choices, press Enter.
      (Type &date, &time, and &page, or choose std page headings.)

    Print standard
      page headings  . . . . .   Y            Y=Yes, N=No

    Page heading
  Vendor Master Penalty Report        By Janie@query.com



    Page footing
  Prepared for Accounting


  F3=Exit          F5=Report          F10=Process/previous
   F12=Cancel       F13=Layout          F18=Files
```

Headers and Footers

Just as a cover page, most users care little about report headings and footings when they are building their queries. However, once the query report actually delivers the goods and provides valuable information to the firm, the credibility of the query report may be proportional to its professional appeal. All of a sudden, a nice header or footer matters.

There is nothing like a header and/or footer to add a professional touch to a business report. Query/400 provides both options in the panel shown in Figure 14-6. Just add your header and/or footer information, and press ENTER, and you are brought back to the Select output type and output form.

☐ Hint: If you are following along, it would be a good idea to press F3 to save your query, run it, and prepare for the next option with a COPY query.

Output Type Database

It's been a long time since you saw this panel, so we repeat it for your convenience in Figure 14-7 below:

Figure 14-7, Select Output Type and Output Form

```
                    Select Output Type and Output Form

Type choices, press Enter.

    Output type  . . . . . . . . . .   3      1=Display
                                              2=Printer
                                              3=Database file

    Form of output . . . . . . . . .   1      1=Detail
                                              2=Summary only

    Line wrapping  . . . . . . . . .   N      Y=Yes, N=No
        Wrapping width . . . . . . . .        Blank, 1 378
        Record on one page . . . . . .   N    Y=Yes, N=No

F3=Exit          F5=Report      F10=Process/previous
F12=Cancel       F13=Layout     F18=Files
```

Picking the Output File

If you select option 3 for the Output Type Parameter in the Select
Output Type and Output Form panel above, your query output is
sent to a database file. You may ask, "What database file?" Along
the way to telling Query where to put the file, you get to specify a few
more things to help Query/400 know how to deal with your results.
For this report, for case study purposes, the summary option for
Form of Output should also be taken.

Define Database File

When you press ENTER after selecting option 3, the very next thing
you get is the Define Database File Output display as shown in
Figure 14-6.

Figure 14-6 Define Your Database File Output

```
                    Define Database File Output

  Type choices, press Enter.
     (The printed definition shows the output file record layout.)

  File . . . . . . . .    QQRYOUT     Name, F4 for list
     Library . . . . .     HELLO      Name, F4 for list
  Member . . . . . . .    *FILE       Name, *FIRST, *FILE, F4 for list
                                                                      Data
  in file . . . . .   1              1=New file, 2=Replace file
                                     3=New member, 4=Replace member
                                     5=Add to member
  For a new file:
     Authority . . . . .  *LIBCRTAUT    *LIBCRTAUT, auth listname,
                                        *CHANGE, *ALL, *EXCLUDE, *USE
     Text . . . . . . .  Query QuikCourse Summary Database
  Print definition . . .  N             Y=Yes, N=No


  F3=Exit         F4=Prompt       F5=Report     F10=Process/previous
  F12=Cancel      F13=Layout      F18= Files
```

In the Define Database File Output panel shown in Figure I-74, you
select the name of the library and the output file to hold the report.
Leave all of the other options default. I don't recall ever changing any
of these options for a new Query. When the panel is filled as in
Figure I-74, give a good press on the ENTER key.

QQRYOUT is the default file name. If this is a Query report database that you want to keep, you should choose a different name before hitting ENTER since, more than likely, there is already a report out there called QQRYOUT which you will write over. Additionally, the next time someone does a database Query to this library, the current Query definition if it is stored as QQRYOUT will be overlaid. The Query report, which in this case is a summary Query, is written to the database later in this process, when you actually run the Query.

When you have completed all of the options on the Define the Query panel, you will run the query. At that time, the report is written to the database file. For the curious Query user, the next logical step, after running the query, is to find the query output in the database file, and look at it to assure it is correct. A snapshot of the database for VENDORP summary report, as taken by DFU, is shown in Figure 14-7.

Figure 14-7 Summary Data In Output Database

```
WORK WITH DATA IN A FILE            Mode . . . . :    CHANGE
Format . . . . :    QQRY            File . . . . :    QQRY

*RECNBR:                 1
BREAK LEVEL:    1
OVERFLOW FLAG:
STATE:          GA
BALOWE TOTAL:          754200
BALOWE AVG:       754200
BALOWE MIN:       754200
BALOWE MAX:       754200
BALOWE COUNT:         1
PENLTY TOTAL:         150840
PENLTY AVG:       150840
PENLTY MIN:       150840
PENLTY MAX:       150840
PENLTY COUNT:         1


F3=Exit                 F5=Refresh      F6=Select format
F9=Insert               F10=Entry       F11=Change
```

☐ Note: Please note that we are jumping ahead here and have run this query without yet showing you how to do so. The objective at this point is to demonstrate how to look at the database output when it is produced during the run. However, in this case study, we have not run the query yet. Unless you already know how to run a query, the fact that we have database output at this time should be somewhat of a mystery for you. This diversion is for instructional purposes only and not to enhance the VENDORP case study.

Use DFU to See File Data

The panel in Figure 14-6 uses IBM's Data File Utility (DFU) to dip into the database file to show the shape of the summary output data, as well as to look at the contents of the first record. It is useful to note that Query does a nice job with output database files.

The way to use DFU to see this file is as follows:

1.   **Type STRDFU and ENTER**
2.   **Option 5 - Update data using temporary program**
3.   **File Name - VENDORP**
4.   **Library Name - HELLO**
5.   **Member name - VENDORP**

What Does the Database Option Do?

It takes the database information that the programmers and analysts pack into the underlying databases which are queried in a detail mode, and it writes those field names and field descriptors to the database file which it creates. Thus, the file which Query/400 puts out, can also be queried with Query/400, since it is a bonafide and complete database file.

What Does DFU Do?

As you can see in the DFU snapshot, Query/400 also does a nice job with summary data, which it writes to the database file. Notice the STATE column heading. It comes from the database. Query/400 however, uses the names of the summary functions as the field names in the output database for this summary-only example. Thus, the summary fields are properly identified in the output database.

Detailed and Summary Query Reports

Both the detailed and summary forms of database file output are substantially different from displayed or printed output. For your edification, you may note the following differences:

Detailed Output to Database

Any report break and summary function output you may have specified are ignored. The query does not bomb. However, only the selected records are put in the database file. Any line wrapping you may specify is ignored.

Summary Output to Database

Query puts basically the same information into a database file as it would put on the report or the display. Each of the fields, such as count, average, max, etc. are placed in the file as database fields for each summary record and final total record produced by the query. A quick DFU look at the file is shown in Figure 14-7.

Form of Output

In the Query Output Type section, we have already demonstrated the detail of the sequence of panels to complete a Query display, printed report, or database output. For continuity purposes, we followed through with all of the panels for the various output types.

However, before you would actually have hit the ENTER key in the Select output type and output form panel, shown again in Figure 14-8, you would have to complete the Form of output and Line wrapping sections.

Figure 14-8, Select Output Type and Output Form

```
                    Select Output Type and Output Form
Type choices, press Enter.

    Output type  . . . . . . . . . .    1      1=Display
                                               2=Printer
                                               3=Database file

    Form of output . . . . . . . . .    1      1=Detail
                                               2=Summary only

    Line wrapping  . . . . . . . . .    N      Y=Yes, N=No
      Wrapping width . . . . . . . .           Blank, 1 378
      Record on one page . . . . . .    N      Y=Yes, N=No

F3=Exit          F5=Report      F10=Process/previous
F12=Cancel       F13=Layout     F18=Files
```

Summary or Detailed

Moving from the Output type prompt to the Form of output prompt, you begin to complete the mid portion of the panel in Figure 14-8. Using this option, you choose whether your report is put out in detail or summary form. In detail form (option 1), you get all the line items in both the printer, display, and database options. In summary form (option 2), you do not see the detail lines, only the summary information.

Line Wrapping

The last section on the Select output type and output form panel refers to Line Wrapping. You would type a "Y" or "N" in this section, as shown in Figure 14-8, to indicate whether lines of the printed report or displayed report are to be wrapped whenever all the fields in the output record cannot fit on one line of the report. Line wrapping is handy if you want to see everything about a record in a report without having to window or scroll or get another sheet of paper. However, it can make a report appear cluttered

Wrapping Length.

If you select wrapping, you can also specify the wrapping record length, which can be up to column 378. If all of the fields of an output record cannot fit within the specified width of one line of the report, the field that would exceed the specified width is started on the next line. If you leave this prompt blank, wrapping occurs whenever the maximum width of the specified display, or printer is reached. Wrapping is not an option for database files.

Record on One Page

Sometimes, though not in the VENDORP case study, you may be storing huge records of information for various entities such as, perhaps Human Resources. Tons of information may be stored in just one record. It may be handy, in such instances, to ask Query to print one record per page, so that the complete record of an individual would not be combined at the top of a page or bottom of a page with the record of another.

Instead of an "N," if you want all of each record to be on the same page in the report, you would type "Y." In this case, as you would expect, text would also be wrapped, rather than have the system trying to display information in columns which do not exist.

Wrapping Up the Output Choices

When you have finished all of the options on the Select output type and output form panel, you can hit ENTER until you return to the main Query panel, Define the Query, as shown in figure 14-9.

Figure 14-9 Define The Query- Output Type & Form Completed

```
                            Define the Query
Query . . . . . . :    FIRSTQ          Option . . . . . :    CREATE
Library . . . . :     HELLO          CCSID . . . . . . :      37
Type options, press Enter.  Press F21 to select all.
  1=Select

Opt     Query Definition Option
      > Specify file selections
      > Define result fields
      > Select and sequence fields
      > Select records
      > Select sort fields
      > Select collating sequence
      > Specify report column formatting
      > Select report summary functions
      > Define report breaks
   1  > Select output type and output form
        Specify processing options

   F3=Exit          F5=Report          F12=Cancel
   F13=Layout       F18=Files          F21=Select all
```

As you can see in Figure 14-9, Query/400 has marked the option with a completed sign ("\>"), which tells you that you have worked this option, and it may be complete.

Now, let's go to Chapter 15, to see what we need to finish up all of the options on this menu, so that we can soon save our query and run it.

Chapter 15   Specify Processing Options

Are We Done Yet?

So, now you have defined a query. You have also used the F5 display option several times to observe your query report as it was being built. You have used all printer options, and you have selected a database option to store your summary results. Of course, one query alone cannot do all of those functions. For each of the option combinations, as you have presumed, you would need a separate query definition.

Anyway, it sure seems like we have already done it all! What else can be left? As you continue your journey down the Define the Query panel first shown in Figure 3-5, and shown below in Figure 15-1, you will notice that there is just one option left - Specify processing options. Once this option is completed, you are finished with your query definition. The VENDORP case study is just about ready to run.

So, to complete our trip, let's take that last option by placing a "1" next to it and pressing ENTER. From here, you will be taken to the Specify Processing Options menu, as shown in Figure 15-2.

Figure 15-1 Define The Query- Select Processing Options

```
                            Define the Query
Query . . . . . . :    FIRSTQ           Option . . . . . :    CREATE
Library . . . . :      HELLO        CCSID . . . . . . :      37
Type options, press Enter.  Press F21 to select all.
  1=Select

Opt     Query Definition Option
      > Specify file selections
      > Define result fields
      > Select and sequence fields
      > Select records
      > Select sort fields
      > Select collating sequence
      > Specify report column formatting
      > Select report summary functions
      > Define report breaks
      > Select output type and output form
   1    Specify processing options

 F3=Exit          F5=Report          F12=Cancel
F13=Layout        F18=Files          F21=Select all
```

Figure 15-2 Specify Processing Options For Query

```
                       Specify Processing Options
Type choices, press Enter.

  Use rounding . . . . . . . . . .          Blank, Y=Yes, N=No

  Ignore decimal
    data errors  . . . . . . . . .          Blank, Y=Yes, N=No

  Ignore character
    substitution warnings  . . . . .   Y    Y=Yes, N=No

  Use collating sequence for
    all character comparisons  . . .   Y    Y=Yes, N=No

 F3=Exit          F5=Report          F10=Process/previous
F12=Cancel        F13=Layout         F18=Files
```

Processing Options

There are four processing options which can be specified in Figure 15-2. They are as follows:

Rounding

You type a "Y" or "N" to indicate whether you want Query/400 to round the results of calculations (results fields and totals) and length changes done on numeric fields when this query is being run. With rounding, results can be quite different than not rounding, depending on what is done, particularly if multiple steps of calculations are performed (rounding at each step) before the final result is stored in the field.

If you decide to leave this prompt blank, the environment that Query/400 run in determines whether rounding is to be performed. For example, rounding is not performed in the System/36 environment, but it is performed in the OS/400 and System/38 environments.

Ignore Decimal Errors

You type a "Y" or "N" to indicate whether you want Query/400 to ignore any decimal data errors it finds in a packed or zoned field when this query is being run. Decimal errors occur for a number of reasons, but often the cause is blank or other invalid data that is stored in a numeric field in the database.

If the data is blank, developers sometimes circumvent the problem by telling the system to treat the blanks as zeroes (ignore decimal errors). However, such errors can also mean that there are more serious issues, such as data alignment problems that would invalidate the results of the query if the errors were ignored. The typical Query user would be advised to leave this switch off, and report any data errors to the IT department, rather than risk the integrity of the report by ignoring them.

If you leave this prompt blank, the operating environment that the query is run in determines whether decimal data errors are to be ignored. Decimal data errors are ignored in the System/36 environment, but they are not ignored in the OS/400 and System/38 environments.

Ignore Character Substitution

This prompt lets you specify whether or not character substitution warnings should be ignored when converting data or an alternative collating table from one coded character set identifier (CCSID), to another. The default is "Y." This means that the query should ignore the substitutions. If you code this value as "N," it means that an error occurs in the query if a substitution should be made. The recommendation is to go with the default value.

Use Collating Sequence

You type "Y" (Yes) or "N" (No) to specify whether the collating sequence you selected via the Collating Sequence option in the Define the Query should be used for EQ, NE, LIST, NLIST, LIKE, and NLIKE character comparisons, in addition to sequencing. This option is ignored when you use the default hexadecimal (EBCDIC) collating sequence. If you have gone though the trouble of building a collating table in this query, this gives you the opportunity to turn it off and on, to help assure your results.

In this case study, and in most practical exercises with Query/400, the processing option you will use the processing option defaults. There is little reason to change them. Most Queries I have observed do not ever get the ">" completed sign on this menu option. Query users find it not worth their bother.

If we did change anything on this menu, however, when we hit the ENTER key, we would return to the Define the Query panel. as shown in Figure 15-3.

Figure 15-3 Define The Query- All Options Completed

```
                          Define the Query
Query . . . . . . :    FIRSTQ          Option . . . . . :    CREATE
Library . . . . :     HELLO           CCSID . . . . . . :    37
 Type options, press Enter.  Press F21 to select all.
   1=Select

Opt    Query Definition Option
     > Specify file selections
     > Define result fields
     > Select and sequence fields
     > Select records
     > Select sort fields
     > Select collating sequence
     > Specify report column formatting
     > Select report summary functions
     > Define report breaks
     > Select output type and output form
     > Specify processing options


  F3=Exit           F5=Report         F12=Cancel
 F13=Layout         F18=Files         F21=Select all
```

As you can see in Figure 15-3, Query/400 has marked the last option with a completed sign (">"), which tells you that you have worked this option and all other options. Your query definition is now complete.

From this panel, remember that you can go back to any of the previously completed options and make any final adjustments to the VENDORP case study before you are finished. For now, I'd say we are done. It's time to head to Chapter 16, so that we can close up the query, save it, and hit the bricks.

Chapter 16   Ending Your Query Session

Heading For Home

When you have finished preparing your query, and you would like to execute it, and perhaps exit Query/400 at the same time, this is the path you will take. From whatever step you may be in, close it out with the ENTER key or F3 or F12, and return to the Defne the Query panel, as shown in Figure 15-3.

As you look at the panel in Figure 15-3, you will notice that each option has a greater-than sign. As you complete each query definition option, you may recall that Query/400 places a greater-than sign ">" next to the option if you have selected it in building your query, and you have changed it from its default.

Exiting and Saving Your Query Definition

As you can see from this panel, you have done it all. It's time to get out, execute your query, and end your Query session. Start this process by pressing F3. You will see the panel as shown in Figure 16-1.

Figure 16-1 Exit, Save, and Run Query Options

```
                         Exit this Query

Type choices, press Enter.

  Save definition  . . .   Y                Y=Yes, N=No

  Run option . . . . . .   1                1=Run interactively
                                            2=Run in batch
                                            3=Do not run

  For a saved definition:
    Query  . . . . . . .   FIRSTQ           Name
       Library  . . . . .  HELLO            Name, F4 for list

    Text . . . . . . . .   The VENDORP First Query FOr this QuikCOurse
    Authority  . . . . .   *CHANGE          *LIBCRTAUT, authorization
                                            listname, *CHANGE, *ALL,
                                            *EXCLUDE, *USE



F4=Prompt        F5=Report         F12=Cancel         F13=Layout
F14=Define the query
```

Selecting F3 from the definition menu sends you on the path to exit.
The questions on the panel in Figure 16-1 have to do with what you
want to do before you exit the query definition phase. If you are not
ready for the exit at this time, you can also undo your exit request by
pressing F12.

Save Definition

The first question is: Do you want to save all of the work you just
completed? I always answer this "Y." If I later choose to free the
system of the space used to save this definition, I delete the query
definition at that time.

Run Option

The next question is: Do you want to run this query at all,
interactively, or in batch mode? As you can see in the display, these
options are lined up nicely as follows right under Run option – after
the Save prompt:

1. = **Run interactively**
2. = **Run in batch**
3. = **Do not run**

Option 3 Do Not Run

You would pick option 3 if you want to save your definition to run later. Perhaps you may have a really large query that should be run at night or on the weekend.

Option 1 Run Interactively

You would pick option 1 if you think you've got a reasonably small query, and you need to get the results right away. Depending on your output – printer, database or display, the results of the query will be available almost immediately.

Option 2 Run in Batch

You would pick option 2 if your query does not have to run immediately. If you can wait a little bit, most of the time, or if you can wait a few hours sometimes, depending on the performance characteristics of your system, this is the preferred option.

Running in batch is much better for the system. It uses the extended processor capabilities of newer AS/400 and iSeries models. For example, a system may have ten or more times the batch computing power than interactive power available for your Query job. When you choose to interactively run a Query job, your queries will run slower, and they will compromise the performance of other work on the system. Printed Query reports and database output from Query are both batch by nature, so they should run in batch. Otherwise, you are sub-optimizing the over-all performance of your machine. Display output must run interactively

Save Name

More than likely, after all that work, you will save your definition with a unique name. You specified a name at the start of the VENDORP Query session (FIRSTQ), though for a new Query definition, this is not necessary. However, since it was specified, Query/400 remembers it and prompts you with the name you have previously selected. If the name and library to store the query are okay, as in Figure 16-1, do not change them.

Use Descriptive Text

You can also add some descriptive text, which is highly recommended. Queries very quickly mount up, and when they are not described well, adept query makers choose to make more queries, rather than finding one that fits. This results in many queries, which are saved, but which are never used again. To help avoid this phenomenon, use text judiciously. It will go a long way in helping make your queries re-usable.

Enter, Run, and Exit

When you have filled out the panel in Figure 16-1 to your satisfaction, press the ENTER key to run this query and save the results. More than likely, after your query runs and your results are displayed or captured, you will return to the Work With Queries panel, which we explain in Chapter 17. At this point in the case study, you have built and executed the VENDORP query. You are now going to find out what comes after you have built some queries.

Chapter 17   Work With Queries Command (WRKQRY)

After the Query

Let's say that we have picked the options to save our definition, and now it is tomorrow. Funny, it seems like yesterday. Just kidding!

More than likely, the data has changed in the underlying VENDORP database since yesterday. Do you need to change your queries when the data changes? No! You do not! Unless the shape of the data (file rebuilt with different or changed fields) has changed, your queries will be good for almost forever. . . unless IBM does something unexpected like withdraw the Query/400 product.

Use WRKQRY

So, how do you get at those saved queries to change them or to run them. First of all, don't ever use the STRQRY command again. Use the WRKQRY command instead. Get yourself a command line capable screen panel, type in WRKQRY, and hit the ENTER key. When you issue a WRKQRY command, you are taken to a panel like the one in Figure 17-1.

Figure 17-1 Work With Queries First Panel

```
                        Work with Queries

Type choices, press Enter.

   Option  . . . . . .   2            1=Create, 2=Change,
                                      3=Copy, 4=Delete
                                      5=Display, 6=Print def
                                      8=Run in batch, 9=Run
   Query . . . . . . .                Name, F4 for list
      Library . . . . .    HELLO      Name, *LIBL, F4-list


 F3=Exit        F4=Prompt       F5=Refresh       F12=Cancel
                        (C) COPYRIGHT IBM CORP. 1988
```

Lots of Options

You can notice in the Work with Queries panel shown in Figure 17-1 that there are many options. Before you select one, we'll give a one line explanation of each so that you are comfortable in using them:

1.   = Create, create new query definition

2.   = Change, change existing query definition

3.   = Copy, copy an existing definition.
        Used for creating a new Query based on an existing
        Query definition.

4.   = Delete, delete a Query definition.

5.   = Display, display a Query definition

6.   = Print definition, Print a Query definition

7.   = Not available, not used

8.   = Run in batch, submit this Quety to batch vs. interactive.

9.   = Run, run this Query interactively

To use any of these options, type in the option number, the query definition name, and the library name in which the definition is stored. Then press ENTER. If you do not know the name of the query at this point, type in the option and the library, position the cursor to the blank name line, and press the prompt (F4) key. You will get a list of all queries in the library to select from.

Changing a Query

Select a 2 in the panel in Figure 17-1 in order to change your query. Then, press F4 to get a list of all the queries in your library. Since your library is fresh, and you created just one query in this QuikCourse, that is the one you will see when you press ENTER from the panel in Figure 17-1. You will be taken to the panel in Figure 17-2.

Figure 17-2 Work With Queries List Panel

```
                            Work with Queries
 Library . . . . . . .      HELLO        Name, *LIBL, F4 for list
 Subset  . . . . . . .                   Name, generic*
 Position to . . . . . .                 Starting characters

 Type options (and Query), press Enter.
   1=Create   2=Change   3=Copy   4=Delete   5=Display   6=Print
   8=Run in batch   9=Run
 Opt  Query           Text                            Changed
  2
  2   FIRSTQ                                           05/15/02

                                                        Bottom
 F3=Exit        F4=Prompt        F5=Refresh    F11=Display names only
 F12=Cancel     F19=Next group
```

Objective

Our intent for this exercise is to modify the FIRSTQ query, which we completed and saved last chapter. This should be really easy, since it is the only query definition listed for the HELLO library.

Opt Field

When you get to the Work with Queries panel, as in Figure 17-2, you will see that the Opt field comes primed with a "2" on the first line. You can ignore that if you choose– as we did. If you want to create a new query, for example, you can change this to a "1," and enter your query name. If you want to change a query, but you do not want to roll through all the queries that may be in the list, you can leave the OPT field at 2 and, on the blank line, type in the name of an existing query.

In this case, we want to work with the FIRSTQ query, so place a "2" next to it, as in Figure 17-2. When you have the information completed, hit the ENTER key. You will be taken to a panel which looks an awful lot like the Define the Query panel last shown in Figure 15-3, and repeated below as Figure 17-3.

Figure 17-3 Define The Query- From WRKQRY (opt 2)

```
                          Define the Query
Query . . . . . . :    FIRSTQ         Option  . . . . . :    CREATE
Library . . . . :      HELLO          CCSID . . . . . . :    37
  Type options, press Enter.  Press F21 to select all.
    1=Select

Opt    Query Definition Option
       > Specify file selections
       > Define result fields
       > Select and sequence fields
    1  > Select records
       > Select sort fields
       > Select collating sequence
       > Specify report column formatting
       > Select report summary functions
       > Define report breaks
    1  > Select output type and output form
       > Specify processing options

  F3=Exit          F5=Report         F12=Cancel
  F13=Layout       F18=Files         F21=Select all
```

Modify the Query

From the Define the Query panel, as you know, you can place a "1" next to any of the options you want to modify. Since you are already trained in each of these options, modifying the query at this point should not be a tough task.

Note: For this QuikCourse, let's say we no longer want the $400.00 bogey for selection, and we want a detailed report to the display. Let's first remove the record selection, and take all of the records.

From the panel in Figure 17-3, place a "1" in the fourth option (Select records,) and you can also place a "1" in the second to last option (Select output type and output form.) Then, press ENTER. You will first see the panel as shown in Figure 17-4.

Figure 17-4 Select Records - VENDORP Original

```
                         Select Records

Type comparisons, press Enter.   Specify OR to start each new group.
   Tests:  EQ, NE, LE, GE, LT, GT, RANGE, LIST, LIKE, IS, ISNOT...

AND/OR  Field      Test    Value (Field, Number, 'Characters', or ...)
        BALOWE     GT      400.00




                                                           Bottom

 Field          Text                                  Len   Dec
 VNDNBR         VENDOR NUMBER                            5    0
 NAME           NAME                                    25
 ADDR1          ADDRESS LINE 1                          25
 CITY           CITY                                    15
 STATE          STATE                                    2
                                                      More...
 F3=Exit        F5=Report     F9=Insert        F11=Display names only
 F12=Cancel     F13=Layout    F20=Reorganize   F24=More keys
```

Remove Selection Criteria

To remove the selection criteria so that you get all the records, either type over it with blanks, or hit the Field Exit key to blank it out. Your panel should look like the panel shown in Figure 17-4.

Figure 17-4 Select Records - VENDORP Original

```
                        Select Records
 Type comparisons, press Enter.  Specify OR to start each new group.
   Tests:  EQ, NE, LE, GE, LT, GT, RANGE, LIST, LIKE, IS, ISNOT...

 AND/OR  Field     Test   Value (Field, Number, 'Characters', or ...)




                                                            Bottom

 Field           Text                              Len  Dec
 VNDNBR          VENDOR NUMBER                        5    0
 NAME            NAME                                25
 ADDR1           ADDRESS LINE 1                      25
 CITY            CITY                                15
 STATE           STATE                                2
                                                    More...
 F3=Exit         F5=Report    F9=Insert      F11=Display names only
 F12=Cancel      F13=Layout   F20=Reorganize F24=More keys
```

When you are ready to commit, there should no longer any selection statements in the query. Hit the ENTER key, and you will be taken to the Select Output Type and Output Form menu, as shown in Figure 17-5.

Figure 17-5, Output Type and Output Form Original

```
                   Select Output Type and Output Form
 Type choices, press Enter.

   Output type  . . . . . . . . . .   3      1=Display
                                             2=Printer
                                             3=Database file

   Form of output . . . . . . . . .   2      1=Detail
                                             2=Summary only

   Line wrapping  . . . . . . . . .   Y      Y=Yes, N=No
     Wrapping width . . . . . . . .          Blank, 1 378
     Record on one page . . . . . .   N      Y=Yes, N=No

 F3=Exit         F5=Report    F10=Process/previous
 F12=Cancel      F13=Layout   F18=Files
```

Change to Display Output

When you come into this menu, the old options for output to a Database file, Summary only, and Line wrapping — are all there, as seen in the panel in Figure 17-5. Change these options to Display, Detail, and no-wrap, as shown in
Figure 17-5. Your panel should now look like Figure 17-6.

Figure 17-6, Output Type and Output Form Modified

```
                        Select Output Type and Output Form
Type choices, press Enter.

    Output type  . . . . . . . . . .   1      1=Display
                                              2=Printer
                                              3=Database file

    Form of output . . . . . . . . .   1      1=Detail
                                              2=Summary only

    Line wrapping  . . . . . . . . .   N      Y=Yes, N=No
      Wrapping width . . . . . . . .           Blank, 1 378
      Record on one page . . . . . .   N      Y=Yes, N=No

F3=Exit          F5=Report      F10=Process/previous
F12=Cancel       F13=Layout     F18=Files
```

When you have this panel completed, hit ENTER and you will
return to the Define the Query panel. From here, press F3 to exit,
and you will see the exit panel as in Figure 17-7.

Figure 17-7 Exit, Save, and Run Query Options

```
                              Exit this Query
    Type choices, press Enter.

      Save definition  . . .   Y          Y=Yes, N=No
      Run option . . . . . .   1          1=Run interactively
                                          2=Run in batch
                                          3=Do not run
      For a saved definition:
        Query  . . . . . . .   FIRSTQA    Name
          Library  . . . . .   HELLO      Name, F4 for list

        Text . . . . . . . .   The VENDORP Second  Query For this QuikCourse
  croated from the first Query

        Authority  . . . . .   *CHANGE      *LIBCRTAUT, authorization
  listname, *CHANGE, *ALL,
                                              *EXCLUDE, *USE
    F4=Prompt       F5=Report       F12=Cancel       F13=Layout     F14=Define
    the query
```

Save and Run the Changed Query

When you press ENTER on the panel in Figure 17-7, your query will
run interactively, and it will be saved as FIRSTQA, to differentiate it
from the FIRSTQ query, which you created in the VENDORP
examples throughout this book. When the query runs, the output
will come to the display as in Figure 17-8.

Figure 17-8 Detailed Query Report To the Display

```
                           Display Report
Query . . . :   HELLO/FIRSTQA            Report width . . . . . :     135
Position to line . . . . .          Shift to column . . . . . .
Line
....+....1....+....2....+....3....+....4....+....5....+....6....+....7..
         VENDORVENDOR                   ADDRESS LINE 1              CITY
         NUMBERNAME

000001   00010Thinking Clocks           43 Timestamp Rd            Gottime
000002
000003
000004
000005
000006
000007
000008
000009
000010   00025A MACHINE CORP.           1345 Prill Avenue          Chicago
000011   00030D CONTROLS                45 Fognetta Place          Kernstin
000012   00028C ENGRAVING CO            Pedulllion Avenue          Greghert
000013
000014
                                                                   More...
F3=Exit      F12=Cancel       F19=Left       F20=Right      F21=Split
```

The Detailed Report Looks Summarized?

As you can see in the panel in Figure 17-8, this is a detail report, and
it is on the display. The huge breaks come from the break totals in
between the detail records. When we changed the query, we did not
replace the breaks and the summary functions, so they appear above
after the state of GA, for example, from lines 2 through 9 of the
report. Since the totals are on the right of the report, you don't see
them in this panel, but a quick F20 would bring them into view.

When you hit the ENTER key while reading this Query report, you
will go back to the prompt panel for the WRKQRY function, as
shown in Figure 17–9 below.

Figure 17-9 Return to Work With Queries

```
                        Work with Queries

Type choices, press Enter.

  Option  . . . . . .           1=Create, 2=Change, 3=Copy, 4=Delete
5=Display, 6=Print definition
8=Run in batch, 9=Run              Query . . . . . . .   FIRSTQA
Name, F4 for list                  Library . . . . .       HELLO
Name, *LIBL, F4 for list



F3=Exit     F4=Prompt     F5=Refresh     F12=Cancel
Query option processing completed successfully.
```

Getting Out of a WRKQRY Session

If you happen to take option 2 again, when you hit ENTER, you will
see your old pal, the Define the Query panel in Figure 17-10.

Figure 17-10 Define The Query- From WRKQRY (opt 2)

```
                        Define the Query
Query . . . . . . :    FIRSTQ         Option . . . . . :    CREATE
Library . . . . :      HELLO          CCSID . . . . . . :      37
  Type options, press Enter.  Press F21 to select all.
    1=Select

Opt     Query Definition Option
        > Specify file selections
        > Define result fields
        > Select and sequence fields
          Select records
        > Select sort fields
        > Select collating sequence
        > Specify report column formatting
        > Select report summary functions
        > Define report breaks
        > Select output type and output form
        > Specify processing options

    F3=Exit           F5=Report          F12=Cancel
    F13=Layout        F18=Files          F21=Select all
```

Notice that the ">" is removed from select records, yet it stayed in
the Select output type and output form option, even though we
changed it back to display.

That wraps up WRKQRY. The intent of the WRKQRY exercise
above is so that you are able to work with previously created queries.
That may not always be what you want to do.

What if you just want to run the query you created? That's why there
is a Chapter 18.

Chapter 18   Run Query Command (RUNQRY)

It's Always Tomorrow!

Suppose it is again tomorrow, and you don't want to modify a query. Instead, you want to run the query you just created. You do not need the STRQRY command, and you do not need the WRKQRY command. The RUNQRY command will do just fine.

What is RUNQRY?

A query definition, such as the FIRSTQ and FIRSTQA definitions that you just you just created and saved, is somewhat like a java program. Now, don't start hating it simply because of that. A java program, in what is called byte code form, needs the resources of another facility, such as a java virtual machine, to translate the byte code into executable instructions at run time.

Query Is Like Java?

The query definition called FIRSTQ, which you created in this QuikCourse, is similar to this. Just as java byte code, it cannot run by itself. Just like you cannot call a java byte code program, you cannot call a query definition. However, a java virtual machine can run a java program. Likewise, a query processor, namely the RUNQRY command, can run your Query program.

Let's examine the panel in Figure 18-1 to get a good look at the command parameters of the RUNQRY command.

Figure 18-1 RUNQRY (Run Query) Command

```
                        Run Query (RUNQRY)

Type choices, press Enter.

Query . . . . . . . . .                Name, *NONE
  Library . . . . . .     *LIBL        Name, *LIBL, *CURLIB
Query file:
  File . . . . . . . . .                Name, *SAME
    Library . . . . . .   *LIBL        Name, *RUNOPT, *LIBL,
*CURLIB
  Member . . . . . . .   *FIRST        Name, *RUNOPT, *FIRST,
*LAST
         + for more values
Report output type . . .  *RUNOPT      *RUNOPT, *DISPLAY...
Output form . . . . . .   *RUNOPT      *RUNOPT, *DETAIL, *SUMMARY
Record selection . . . .  *NO          *NO, *YES


                                                     Bottom
F3=Exit  F4=Prompt  F5=Refresh F12=Cancel F13=How to display
F24=More keys
```

Query Name and Library

The Query name and library are easy enough to handle. Since you have but one query at this point, you would fill this in as FIRSTQ and HELLO. The Query file name and library for the query are not always needed, but they are needed in these two cases:

1.   If you decide to run this same FIRSTQ query against a different, yet similar file.

2.   If you do not specify a query name.

For fully defined queries, in which you are not making file name changes, the query file name is not needed. For the VENDORP case study, leave it blank.

Query Fast Path

How can you have a run query command which has no query definition? We said previously in this chapter that just as java byte code needs a java virtual machine to interpret it, so it can execute, a query definition needs a RUNQRY command to execute. However, a RUNQRY command can do fine without a query definition. It can actually build a query definition on the fly.

The ultimate query fast path is the RUNQRY with no query definition name. With no named definition, what can the RUNQRY query? It can query the file name specified in the RUNQRY command!

Obviously, in this case, all fields are selected, but there is a Select Records parameter which we discuss below. It is a reasonably powerful, yet simple and phenomenally quick way to get a nice, neat, and complete database file listing. You can even get a partial list based on record selection.

Other RUNQRY Options

There are three options after the file selection which deserve your attention. Let's look at them individually.

Report Output Type

Specifies where the report or output produced by the query is sent. The options below are certainly germane to the undefined query, as noted above, but you can also override a query originally defined for a particular output designation, such as a printer, and send it to a display. As one would expect, if no value is specified in the query, and no value is entered on the command, or if a query name is not specified for the command, *DISPLAY is assumed.

The possible values for this option are as follows:

*RUNOPT

If a query definition is being used, the type of output specified in the query definition is the type of output produced when this query is run.

*DISPLAY
The output produced by the query is sent to the display station that runs the command. If you submit the RUNQRY command with the

*DISPLAY option, however, since batch jobs have no display associated, the output is sent to the printer instead of the display.

*PRINTER.

The output produced by the query is printed. The command will expand to ask pertinent questions about the printout, though not as many questions as are asked in the query definition.

*OUTFILE.

The output is directed to a database file. With intelligent prompting, the RUNQRY command opens up after this selection is made and asks the questions necessary to create the output database file from the information requested.

Output Form

You specify the form of output produced by the query - either *detail or *summary. This gives you the opportunity to override your original query definition. If no value is specified in the query, and no value was entered on the command, or if a query name is not specified, *DETAIL is assumed.

Record Selection

You specify whether or not you want this query run with a run time selection. In other words, during the RUNQRY command, Query/400 stops and gives you the same record selection, as in Query definition (Figure 17-4).

Since the QUERY/400 product is actually creating a definition at that point, IBM cautions that the AS/400 Query/400 licensed program must be installed and the Query must be run interactively in order to be able to specify *YES to the record selection criteria. If no selection is necessary, specify *NO.

That's almost all folks

It's time to toughen up and move on to the more complex. In Chapter 19, you are introduced to a new JOIN case study. It's really VENDORP with some bells and whistles for your enjoyment. Let's go there now.

Chapter 19. Join Case Study

Why Join?

We would not be doing you a service if we ended this book without
working through a Join example. Join is a very powerful relational
operator used to take pieces of related records in one file and combine
them with pieces of related records in another file. The typical need
for a Join comes about when transactions are in one file and text
descriptions are in another file, and there is a common field by which
the files can be linked.

Simple Join Definition by Example

A General Ledger (GL) journal entry file would be a good example.
The account number, date of transaction, and amount, would be
three of the key fields in the journal file. If this file were listed in a
query report, there would be little information that could be gained
without having a list of the account numbers and the names of the
accounts. This list would help you know, for example, that Account
1000 for example is for Cash and that account # 1100 is for
Accounts Receivable, etc.

Wouldn't it be nice if you could combine the two files, so that ,for
each journal transaction, it would automatically go to the Chart of
Accounts file to pick up the account name? Of course it would!
Fortunately, that is exactly what the Join facility in the Query/400
product provides.

The Join Method

The way you do this is by selecting both files and declaring a common field, such as account number, that can be used to link the two files during the query run. The objective is to use the account number field in both files, the account name from the Chart of Accounts Master File, and the date and dollar amount from the Journal Transaction File. When the account numbers match, the Query/400 product takes the information from both files, joins it, and provides a joined record format including account#, name, date, and dollar amount in the query report.

The Advanced VENDORP/ITEMP Case Study

In this case study, you will join two files, the VENDORP file, with which you are already most familiar, and the ITEMP file which is described in Figure 19-1.

Figure 19-1 Item File For Join Case Study

```
Columns . . . :    1  71              Edit              HELLO/QDDSSRC
SEU==>                                                  ITEMP
FMT PF
.....A..........T.Name+++++RLen++TDpB......Functions++++++++++++++++++
          ************** Beginning of data ********************************
001.00     A    R ITEMMSTR                  TEXT('VENDORP  DB FORMAT')
002.00     A      VNDNBR      5S 0           COLHDG('VENDOR' 'NUMBER')
003.00     A                                 ALIAS(VENDOR_NUMBER)
004.00     A      ITNO        6S 0           COLHDG('ITEM' 'NUMBER')
005.00     A      ITDESC     25              COLHDG('ITEM DESCRIPTION')
006.00     A                                 ALIAS(ITEM_DESCRIPTION)
          ************* End of data *********************************************

F3=Exit   F4=Prompt   F5=Refresh   F9=Retrieve   F10=Cursor   F11=Toggle
F16=Repeat find       F17=Repeat change          F24=More keys
                            (C) COPYRIGHT IBM CORP. 1981, 2000.      :
```

Define the Report

Since the ITEMP file description, as shown in Figure 19-1, has no vendor description, a Join with VENDORP is in order. The Join operation is an ideal way of combining the data from the VENDORP file which holds the vendor name, with the item file which contains the item description. The report you would request has just four fields as follows:

Field	File
Vendor number	**ITEMP**
Item number	**ITEMP**
Vendor name	**VENDORP**
Item description	**ITEMP**

The report should be sequenced on Item number, within Vendor number.

Well, now that the query is designed , let's get it done. The first and most tricky part of a Join is to get the files defined to the Query/400 program itself. Since the item file (ITEMP) is the primary file for this Join (we want the vendor name for items), you should define it first to the query. After you specify the ITEMP file, in order to get the next file, you press the F9 key. T hen, you can add the definition of the VENDORP file to the mix for the Join.

Case Study from Scratch

By the way, you will not be continuing the VENDORP case study, so none of this work has been done. This case study is from scratch.

Start the process by using the WRKQRY command. Type WRKQRY, and press ENTER. Select the Create a new query option (1) and press ENTER. Name your query JOIN1, and store it in the HELLO library. You will get the Define the Query panel as in Figure 19-2.

Figure 19-2 Define The Query - File Selections

```
                         Define the Query
Query . . . . . . :    FIRSTQ          Option  . . . . . :    CREATE
Library . . . . :    HELLO            CCSID . . . . . . :    37
Type options, press Enter.  Press F21 to select all.
  1=Select

Opt    Query Definition Option
  1    Specify file selections
       Define result fields
       Select and sequence fields
       Select records
       Select sort fields
       Select collating sequence
       Specify report column formatting
       Select report summary functions
       Define report breaks
       Select output type and output form
       Specify processing options

  F3=Exit          F5=Report         F12=Cancel
  F13=Layout       F18=Files         F21=Select all
```

Specify Join Files

You may recall from the beginning of the first case study that, whenever you create a query, the system automatically selects the first option, as shown in the panel in Figure 19-2. In order to define the files for the Join query, all you have to do at this point is press ENTER.

The panel is already primed to give you the File Selection screen when you hit ENTER. This File Selection panel is shown in Figure 19-3.

Figure 19-3 Specify First Files for Join

```
                         Specify File Selections

Type choices, press Enter.  Press F9 to specify an additional
  file selection.

  File . . . . . . . . .                  Name, F4 for list
     Library  . . . . . .    HELLO        Name, *LIBL, F4 for list
  Member . . . . . . . .    *FIRST        Name, *FIRST, F4 for list
  Format . . . . . . . .    *FIRST        Name, *FIRST, F4 for list




  F3=Exit          F4=Prompt        F5=Report         F9=Add file
  F12=Cancel       F13=Layout       F24=More keys
  Select file(s), or press Enter to confirm.
```

Defining the First File - ITEMP

When you first arrive at this panel, the File Selection panel looks very similar to Figure 19-3. On this panel, type in the ITEMP file name as follows, and hit the ENTER key.

File . . .   ITEMP
Library . .   HELLO

You will be taken to a panel that looks very similar to that in Figure 19-4.

Figure 19-4 Specify First Files for Join

```
                        Specify File Selections

Type choices, press Enter.  Press F9 to specify an additional
    file selection.

    File . . . . . . . . .    ITEMP        Name, F4 for list
       Library  . . . . . .       HELLO    Name, *LIBL, F4 for list
    Member . . . . . . .      *FIRST       Name, *FIRST, F4 for list
    Format . . . . . . .      ITEMMSTR     Name, *FIRST, F4 for list

F3=Exit           F4=Prompt        F5=Report           F9=Add file
F12=Cancel        F13=Layout       F24=More keys
Select file(s), or press Enter to confirm.
```

Defining the Second File - VENDORP

If your intention were to use one file in this query, you would hit ENTER, and proceed with the rest of the definition. However, since this is a Join query, you need to specify the next file for the Join. To tell Query/400 to give you the space to type in the information for the VENDORP file, press F9. A panel similar to that in Figure 19-5 will appear.

Figure 19-5 Specify Next File for Join

```
                        Specify File Selections
Type choices, press Enter.  Press F9 to specify an additional
   file selection.

   File . . . . . . . . .   ITEMP          Name, F4 for list
      Library . . . . . .       HELLO      Name, *LIBL, F4 for list
   Member . . . . . . . .   *FIRST         Name, *FIRST, F4 for list
   Format . . . . . . . .   ITEMMSTR       Name, *FIRST, F4 for list
   File ID . . . . . . .    T01  <<<       A Z99, *ID

   File . . . . . . . . .                  Name, F4 for list
      Library . . . . . .       HELLO      Name, *LIBL, F4 for list
   Member . . . . . . . .   *FIRST         Name, *FIRST, F4 for list
   Format . . . . . . . .   *FIRST         Name, *FIRST, F4 for list
   File ID . . . . . . .    *ID            A Z99, *ID

Bottom
  F3=Exit           F4=Prompt         F5=Report         F9=Add file
  F12=Cancel        F13=Layout        F24=More keys
```

Four things will have happened when you hit F9 in this example:

1.   The most obvious is that you now have the space to type the VENDORP file name (under File ID - T01).

2.   The second thing is that Query/400 went inside the ITEMP file and brought back the format name (ITEMMSTR) to replace the *First parameter.

3.   The third is that Query/400 added a line to the first file and called it File ID and primed the field with T01.

4.   The fourth thing is that under the Format prompt for the second file (last prompt line), Query/400 added a second File ID prompt and primed it with *ID.

After these four Query/400 actions, it is your turn again. For the second file, type in the VENDORP file name as follows, and then hit the ENTER key.

File . . .   VENDORP
Library . . .   HELLO

Completed Join File Definitions

When you hit ENTER, you are taken to a panel that looks very similar to that in Figure 19-6.

Figure 19-6 Completed Files For Join

```
                    Specify File Selections
Type choices, press Enter.  Press F9 to specify an additional
  file selection.

    File . . . . . . . . .   ITEMP        Name, F4 for list
      Library  . . . . . .     HELLO      Name, *LIBL, F4 for list
    Member . . . . . . . .   *FIRST       Name, *FIRST, F4 for list
    Format . . . . . . . .   ITEMMSTR     Name, *FIRST, F4 for list
    File ID  . . . . . . .   T01          A Z99, *ID

    File . . . . . . . . .   VENDORP      Name, F4 for list
      Library  . . . . . .     HELLO      Name, *LIBL, F4 for list
    Member . . . . . . . .   *FIRST       Name, *FIRST, F4 for list
    Format . . . . . . . .   VNDMSTR      Name, *FIRST, F4 for list
    File ID  . . . . . . .   T02          A Z99, *ID


Bottom
F3=Exit         F4=Prompt        F5=Report          F9=Add file
F12=Cancel      F13=Layout       F24=More keys
Select file(s), or press Enter to confirm.
```

Two things happen to the File Selection panel after you type in the second file name (VENDORP) and you press ENTER:

1.   Query/400 goes into the VENDORP file within IBMi and finds the first format name (VNDMSTR), spells it out, and replaces the term *FIRST as shown in Figure 19-6.

2.   The second thing is that, under the Format prompt for the second file (last prompt line), Query/400 changed the File ID response to T02.

What is a File ID?

The File ID comes with the Join. The system knows that since you have specified more than one file, field selections will be coming from two files. Query/400 assigned the first file with an ID of T01 and, after we typed the information for VENDORP and hit ENTER, Query/400 changed the *ID parameter to T02.

Thus, when you move to field selection in the Define the Query menu, you use this IBMi Query created ID to select specific fields from one or the other files (ITEMP or VENDORP). The File ID provides a consistent shorthand notation for the files. In this example, T01 refers to the ITEMP file, and T02 refers to the VENDORP file.

When your panel looks like the one in Figure 19-6, you are finished with file selections. Press ENTER until you see a panel similar to that in Figure 19-7.

Figure 19-7 Specify the Type of Join For the Query

```
                        Specify Type of Join

 Type choice, press Enter.

   Type of join . . . . . . .   1     1=Matched records
                                      2=Matched records with primary file
                                      3=Unmatched records with primary file




 F3=Exit          F5=Report          F10=Process/previous
 F12=Cancel       F13=Layout         F18=Files
```

Specify Type of Join

Now that we picked files, we must tell Query/400 a few more things.

A.   What type of Join are you doing?

1.   Matched records
2.   Match records with primary file
3.   Unmatched records with primary file.

B.   What Fields are used to provide the link for the Join?

Now, lets look at the three Join types in some level of detail.

Join Opt. 1 – Matched Records

These are typical Join options. In our case study, we have typed just four item records into the ITEMP file. We also know that there are vendor records for those four item records. We know that there are no missing vendor records today. Therefore, our best option is option 1. If there are no vendor records for an item, then, for this query, you do not want to see the item records. Another name for this is a matched join or inner join.

Join Opt. 2 -Match Records w/ Primary File.

When you match records with the primary file, you are performing a left outer join. It gives all the records in the primary file (left file), even if there is no matched secondary for a given record. The system plugs default values into the secondary field name slots in the joined query record. Since we are looking for vendor name from the secondary file, not a default value, this facility adds little value to this query, so we do not select this option.

Join Opt. 3 Unmatched Recs w/ Pri File

The Unmatched Records with Primary File option gives a list of only the primary records which have no matching secondaries. This can help a database administrator assure that all matches that should be there, are in fact present. If they are not, the option 3 type of match will show the primary records which are in error. Again, this has no value in the query we are attempting to achieve.

For the case study, type a "1" for a Matched Join, and press ENTER.
You will get the Join specification panel in
Figure 19-8.

Figure 19-8 Join Specification for Query

```
                   Specify How to Join Files

Type comparisons to show how file selections are related, press Enter.
  Tests:  EQ, NE, LE, GE, LT, GT

Field             Test      Field




                                                       Bottom

Field             Text                                  Len
Dec
T01.VNDNBR        VENDOR NUMBER                            5
0
T01.ITNO          ITEM NUMBER                              6
0
T01.ITDESC        ITEM DESCRIPTION                        25
T02.VNDNBR        VENDOR NUMBER                            5
0
T02.NAME          NAME                                    25
                                                       More...
F3=Exit       F5=Report      F10=Process/previous   F11=Display names only
F12=Cancel    F13=Layout     F18=Files              F24=More keys
```

Making The Join

In the Specify How to Join Files panel above (figure 19-8), you
identify the fields that you want to engage for the Join. As you may
recall from earlier panels, T01 refers to the ITEMP file, and T02
refers to the VENDORP file.

On the bottom of the panel, you can see that there are two VNDNBR
fields (vendor number). With the prefix before the field you can tell
that one filed comes from the ITEMP file, and the other comes from
the VENDORP file. These two common fields (VNDNBR) will be
used to Join the two files.

Join Test Operators

From the fifth text line of the panel in Figure 19-8, to the eighth line, you can specify the fields involved in the Join, as well as the type of test to be used. The most common test operator is the equal test. However, the following operations are also available for Joining:

EQ Join if equal
NE Join if not equal
LE Join if less than or equal
GE Join if greater than or equal
LT Join if less than
GT join if greater than

In the Join case study example, as you may recall, the objective is to join file records if the VNDNBR field from the record in the ITEMP file (T01.VNDNBR) is equal to the VNDNBR field in the VENDORP file (T02.VNDNBR).

To perform the coding for this, we borrowed part of the panel from Figure 19-8, and typed the Join criterion as follows:

Field	Test	Field
T01.VNDNBR	**EQ**	**T02.VNDNBR**

This statement reads:

Join the record from the ITEMP file to the record in the VENDORP file when the VNDNBR field from a record in the ITEMP file is equal to the VNDNBR field from a record in the VENDORP file.

When you finish typing the statement, the panel should look like that shown in Figure 19-9.

Figure 19-9 Join Specification for Query

```
                        Specify How to Join Files

Type comparisons to show how file selections are related, press Enter.
   Tests:  EQ, NE, LE, GE, LT, GT

Field               Test    Field
T01.VNDNBR          EQ      T02.VNDNBR
                                                                    Bottom

Field               Text                                            Len
Dec
T01.VNDNBR          VENDOR NUMBER                                     5
0
T01.ITNO            ITEM NUMBER                                       6
0
T01.ITDESC          ITEM DESCRIPTION                                 25
T02.VNDNBR          VENDOR NUMBER                                     5
0
T02.NAME            NAME                                             25
                                                                   More...
F3=Exit        F5=Report      F10=Process/previous   F11=Display names only
F12=Cancel     F13=Layout     F18=Files              F24=More keys
```

Case Study Join Specification

As you can see in Figure 19-9, there are a number of operators which
can be used to form a Join. For example, any of these - EQ, NE, LE,
GE, LT, GT — can be used. If the comparison test is true then the
records are joined. As you can see, the case study uses an EQ Join.

Because Join is considered an advanced topic for Query users, we
again describe the Join process in the example, in different words
below:

The Join Explanation #2

Notice that there are two VNDNBR fields in the field list. That
makes sense since there are two files - ITEMP and VENDORP and
both have the VNDNBR field spelled the same, and both use the
same exact attributes for the field. VNDNBR is the relational key
with which we join these files. You may recall that back at the
bottom of the panel in Figure 19-6, we defaulted to a nickname (T02)
for the secondary file (VENDORP) in the Join. In Figure 19-9, we
use the nickname so that QUERY/400 can differentiate the fields in
ITEMP from those in VENDORP.

How the Join Works

So, for this Join case study, when an ITEMP record is read by the query, and there is a corresponding record in the VENDORP file which matches on VNDNBR, the two records are joined. In other words, if the vendor number in ITEMP– a.k.a T01.VNDNBR is equal to the vendor number field in any VENDORP record – a.k.a. T02.VNDNBR, the record will be joined and presented in the view. That is what the one line of coding in Figure 19-9 provides.

Going Back Home for More

When you hit ENTER from the panel in Figure 19-9, after making this specification, you will come back to the infamous Define the Query panel, which now looks, exactly the same as it did when we started, with the exception that it now has a solo ">" sign on the File Selection option. You have selected th files and provided the Join criteria with this menu option.

Getting the Quick (F5) Report

If you hit F5 right now, you would see the first panel of a wide report as shown in Figure 19-10. You can see that the Join worked, since the vendor name is in the report. Did it really work though?

Figure 19-10 Join Files Connected and Working?

```
                               Display Report
                                     Report width . . . . . :      181
Position to line  . . . . .          Shift to column  . . . . . .
Line
 ....+....1....+....2....+....3....+....4....+....5....+....6....+....7..
         VENDOR   - ITEM     ITEM DESCRIPTION     VENDOR   NAME
         NUMBER     NUMBER                        NUMBER
000001       38    2,000     Buzzard WIngs            38   J B COMPANY
000002       38    3,500     Berinoif Snerds          38   J B COMPANY
000003       44    5,600     Snabber Mungruffs        44   J B EQUIP INC
000004       48      760     Ventricle Carbometer     48   DENTON AND BALL
****** ********  End of report  ********
                                                                 Bottom
F3=Exit      F12=Cancel      F19=Left      F20=Right      F21=Split
```

Did the Join Work?

We had defined our query as having four fields, yet we did not specify any fields. We also said that our query would be sorted on item number within vendor number. Funny, we did none of that, yet that is how the report came out in Figure 19-10.

It's not coincidence. Well, not exactly! Take another look. There are two VENDOR NUMBER columns! How did that happen? We did nothing to prevent it. That's how it happened. We got the VENDOR NUMBER field from both files.

Select Some Fields

Now, let's get it right. Let's go back to the Define the Query menu and pick the Select and sequence fields option by placing a "1" next to it and hitting ENTER. You get the panel in Figure 19-11.

Figure 19-11 Fields Choices for Join Record

```
                    Select and Sequence Fields

 Type sequence number (0 9999) for the names of up to 500 fields to
   appear in the report, press Enter.

 Seq    Field          Text                                      Len
 Dec
        T01.VNDNBR      VENDOR NUMBER                              5
 0
        T01.ITNO        ITEM NUMBER                                6
 0
        T01.ITDESC      ITEM DESCRIPTION                          25
        T02.VNDNBR      VENDOR NUMBER                              5
 0
        T02.NAME        NAME                                      25
        T02.ADDR1       ADDRESS LINE 1                            25
        T02.CITY        CITY                                      15
        T02.STATE       STATE                                      2
        T02.ZIPCD       ZIP CODE                                   5
 0
        T02.VNDCLS      VENDOR CLASS                               2
 0
        T02.VNDSTS      A=ACTIVE, D=DELETE, S=SUSPEND              1
        T02.BALOWE      BALANCE OWED                               9
 2
                                                            More...
   F3=Exit         F5=Report       F11=Display names only  F12=Cancel
   F13=Layout      F20=Renumber        F21=Select all       F24=More keys
```

From the panel in Figure 19-11, select your fields and specify the proper sequence. Be careful not to select VNDNBR twice. Type the four sequence selections as follows:

Seq   Field

1   T01.VNDNBR
2   T01.ITNO
3   T01.ITDESC
    T02.VNDNBR
4   T02.NAME

When you have typed in your field sequence selections, your panel should look like that in Figure 19-12.

Figure 19-12 Select Fields for Join Record

```
                        Select and Sequence Fields

     Type sequence number (0 9999) for the names of up to 500 fields to
       appear in the report, press Enter.

      Seq   Field            Text                                    Len
      Dec
       1    T01.VNDNBR       VENDOR NUMBER                            5
      0
       2    T01.ITNO         ITEM NUMBER                              6
      0
       3    T01.ITDESC       ITEM DESCRIPTION                         25
            T02.VNDNBR       VENDOR NUMBER                            5
      0
       4    T02.NAME         NAME                                     25
            T02.ADDR1        ADDRESS LINE 1                           25
            T02.CITY         CITY                                     15
            T02.STATE        STATE                                    2
            T02.ZIPCD        ZIP CODE                                 5
      0
            T02.VNDCLS       VENDOR CLASS                             2
      0
            T02.VNDSTS       A=ACTIVE, D=DELETE, S=SUSPEND            1
            T02.BALOWE       BALANCE OWED                             9
      2

                                                                More...
       F3=Exit          F5=Report        F11=Display names only  F12=Cancel
       F13=Layout       F20=Renumber     F21=Select all          F24=More keys
```

Fixing the Rest of the Join Query

Take notice that the first five fields in the panel shown in Figure 19-12 are the same first five fields as in the report in Figure 19-10. That explains the phenomenon of two VNDNBR fields. If, in the panel in Figure 19-10, you hit the F20 key, you would see the rest of the fields to the right on the query report. There were lots more than four fields.

Using an F5 query with no field selections gives you all the fields. There are as many fields as exist in both files. We had done nothing to limit the number to the four fields, as prescribed in the initial design. If now, you pick just the four fields as in Figure 19-12, this should do the trick. Our results would look differently.

Press the ENTER key after making the selections as in Figure 19-12. Then, press F5 again, and you will see a panel similar to the one shown in Figure 19-13.

Figure 19-13 Join Report With Four Fields Sorted?

```
                              Display Report
                                  Report width . . . . . :      71
  Position to line  . . . . .     Shift to column  . . . . . .
    Line  ....+....1....+....2....+....3....+....4....+....5....+....6...7.
          VENDOR    ITEM      ITEM DESCRIPTION          NAME
  NUMBER   NUMBER
   000001     38    2,000   Buzzard Wings            J B COMPANY
   000002     38    3,500   Berinof Snerds           J B COMPANY
   000003     44    5,600   Snabber Mungruffs        J B EQUIP INC
   000004     48      760   Ventricle Carbometer     DENTON AND BALL
   ****** ******** End of report  ********
                                                     Bottom
    F3=Exit      F12=Cancel      F19=Left     F20=Right     F21=Split
```

A Sort Without a Sort?

There, now, that does it... Right? Well, not exactly! We had defined that the report should be in item number, within vendor number sequence. Is it? It certainly is! Well, then what is wrong? If something is wrong, why does it look right?

The answer is that it is wrong, but it is correct. It looks right, because there are only four records in the item master file, and they were typed in vendor number sequence, one after the other. The one instance in which one vendor (38) had two products, the items were also typed in sequence. It just happened that way. There is no key on the item file to arrange the records in any sequence. They are in the report in the arrival sequence of the primary file, which is the ITEMP file.

Use the Sort, Sport!

How can you assure yourself that you always get the report in the correct sequence – even when luck is not on our side, as in Figure 19-13? You need to go back to your Define the Query panel, as in Figure 19-14, and select your sort fields.

Figure 19-14 Selecting Sort Fields For Join Query

```
                      Select Sort Fields

  Type sort priority (0 999) and A (Ascending) or D (Descending) for
    the names of up to 32 fields, press Enter.

  Sort
  Prty A/D  Field          Text                                  Len
  Dec
    1    A   T01.VNDNBR     VENDOR NUMBER                          5
  0
    2    A   T01.ITNO       ITEM NUMBER                            6
  0
             T01.ITDESC     ITEM DESCRIPTION                      25
             T02.NAME       NAME                                  25
                                                               Bottom
  F3=Exit          F5=Report       F11=Display names only  F12=Cancel
  F13=Layout       F18=Files       F20=Renumber            F24=More keys
```

In Figure I-37, pick the vendor number and item number field from the primary file for the sort. This will assure you that no matter what record gets entered next in the item master file, the report query will continue to be in the correct sequence.

When you hit ENTER, and then you hit F5 for a report on your changed Join case study, you won't be surprised. The report looks exactly like that in Figure 19-13.

So much for joining files. That wasn't so bad. You can now save your Query/400 report, quit for the day, read my concluding remarks and relax!

Good Work!

Chapter 20   Summary and Conclusions

According To Many

AS/400 Query, according to IBM and most users simply is flexible, powerful, and easy to use. The fact that it knows about the integrated relational database right from the start helps Query provide its high level of usability right out of the box..

AS/400 Query is a very popular, very nice, green screen interactive AS/400 product. It is very good! However, if IBM were not so concerned about the AS/400 being a GUI machine, Query/400 could already be the front end decision support tool for data warehousing on all platforms, and IBM could be the leader. Instead unfortunately, neither are true.

Speaking of data warehousing, many users try to make effective use of Query products in their shops, but cannot because their data is just not shaped properly. A few years ago, I wrote a book which is still very current, called AS/400 Data Warehousing. It provides the insights to help IT staffs shape data for decision making, not just for production applications. It was available for many years in its second edition at MC Press– http://mc store.com/asdatwar.html. It may not be available there now but I still have a few rare copies. I never took the copyright and created my own book and I never made it available with Lets Go Publish! or Amazon or Kindle like this book.

With properly shaped data, the IBM AS/400 Query product can be even more valuable in providing critical ad hoc reports for decision makers. In addition to the ease with which you can design and run queries using the tools we covered in this QuikCourse, the powerful Work with Queries display enables you to create, change, copy, delete, display, or run one or more queries, and print their definitions.

When a query is run, it selects, formats, and analyzes information from database files and produces a report or another file - your choice. And with the RUNQRY command, even if you did not build a query the way you now want to use it, or if you did not built it at all, you can still override, or specify selection information, at "Run" time. This makes the Query/400 tool even that much more powerful and productive for your organization.

Query/400 is the most used decision support tool for AS/400 and iSeries users. It even provides a big, complicated database capability such like Join, and makes it look like as if it were a piece of cake. There are very few shops who do not use IBM's Query/400 product. Now, if only we could convince IBM of that!

Keep up the good work! I hope to see you in another QuikCourse sometime soon!

The Best!

Appendix A Database Primer for Query/400

Why Learn Database?

#1—and most important--you can't do queries if there is no database. You can't do queries if you have no clue about data. So, let's take the time now, in this optional reading appendix to gain more than a clue's worth of kowledge about data and the AS/400 and IBM i database.

What is Data?

Before we define database, let's define data. Data can be defined simply as a group of unorganized facts. For emphasis, many use the redundant term "raw data" to refer to "data" to accentuate the unorganized nature of the facts. Information, a term often misused in place of data, is data, organized for decision making. Query/400 creates information from data. Through computer processes and database structures, data becomes information.

What is a Database?

A database, then, is an organized collection of data (information) that is necessary to perform a task or application. Related data fields are grouped together into a format called a record. Similar records are grouped together into a file. One or more related data files can be grouped to make up a data base.

What is Data Base Management?

Database Management is the process of managing data. It is the underlying software which enables the database to function. Data Management is needed to provide organization, access, and control of the data that is stored on a computer system.

Tables, Rows, and Columns

The AS/400 is unique in the industry in that it has an integrated relational database. A relational database consists of tables that are perceived to be stored in flat files. They appear to line up in a series of rows and columns, regardless of their true underlying structure. Unlike the complicated structures of databases from the past, this database is conceptually easy to understand, thus making it usable by folks like us, who prefer to let the rocket science to the rocket scientists.

A relational file or table, called a physical file on the AS/400, is composed of rows, which are made up of columns. On the AS/400, we call the rows, records; the columns, fields; and the tables, files. Records from different files can be logically linked together by the data in fields that have natural relationships. For example, the employee number field in the Payroll master (MEMPNO)would have a natural relationship with the employee number field in the Timecard file (TEMPNO). Finally, each record in a well designed database file, has a unique key, a field that uniquely identifies the record. This happens to be called the primary key.

Use DDS to Create File Objects

On AS/400, databases are naturally built using a free language that is implemented using data description specifications (DDS). Programmers use these DDS forms to describe the data to the system. After typing the DDS into the system using SEU, programmers and database administrators when they exist use a command called Create Physical File (CRTPF) to create a database object.

The DDS for the VENDORP (a sample vendor file) was first shown in this book way back in Figure 1-2. The CRTPF is applied to this, set of data as typed and the VENDORP file then gets created in the HELLO library, a special library built by me just for this book. The DDS for a dictionary file named VENDORPA, that has the exact field definitions for the VENDORP file, is shown below in Figure A-1. Please take a look at it.

Figure A-1 File Description (Record Layout) for VENDORP file

```
  Columns . . . :    1   71            Browse
HELLO/QDDSSRC
  SEU==>
VENDORPA
  FMT PF
.....A..........T.Name++++++RLen++TDpB......Functions++++++++++++++++++
          *************** Beginning of data
**************************************
0001.00      A    R VNDMSTR                      TEXT('VENDORP   DB
FORMAT')
0002.00      A        VNDNBR      5S  0          COLHDG('VENDOR' 'NUMBER')
0003.00      A                                   ALIAS(VENDOR_NUMBER)
0004.00      A        NAME        25             COLHDG('NAME')
0005.00      A        ADDR1       25             COLHDG('ADDRESS LINE 1')
0006.00      A                                   ALIAS(ADDRESS_LINE_1)
0007.00      A        CITY        15             COLHDG('CITY')
0008.00      A        STATE        2             COLHDG('STATE')
0009.00      A        ZIPCD        5  0          COLHDG('ZIP''CODE')
0010.00      A                                   ALIAS(ZIP_CODE)
0011.00      A        VNDCLS       2  0          COLHDG('VENDOR' 'CLASS')
0012.00      A                                   ALIAS(VENDOR_CLASS)
0013.00      A        VNDSTS       1             COLHDG('ACTIVE' 'CODE')
0014.00      A                                   ALIAS(ACTIVE_CODE)
0015.00      A                                   TEXT('A=ACTIVE, D=DELETE,
+
0016.00      A                                   S=SUSPEND')
0017.00      A        BALOWE       9  2          COLHDG('BALANCE' 'OWED')
0018.00      A                                   ALIAS(BALANCE_OWED)
0019.00      A        SRVRTG       1             COLHDG('SERVICE'
'RATING')
0020.00      A                                   ALIAS(SERVICE_RATING)
0021.00      A                                   TEXT('G=GOOD, A=AVERAGE,
+
0022.00      A                                   B=BAD, P=PREFERRED')

  F3=Exit    F5=Refresh    F9=Retrieve   F10=Cursor   F11=Toggle   F12=Cancel
  F16=Repeat find          F24=More keys
                                    (C) COPYRIGHT IBM CORP. 1981, 2000.
```

In Chapter 19, we introduced another file called ITEMP for our Join case study. Its DDS are first shown in Figure 19-1. The DDS for the ITEMPA dictionary file used to create the ITEMP object is shown on the next page as Figure A-2.

Figure A-2 Check The ITEMP Record Layout DSPFFD

```
Columns . . . :    1  71            Browse
HELLO/QDDSSRC
 SEU==>
ITEMPA
 FMT PF
.....A..........T.Name++++++RLen++TDpB......Functions++++++++++++++++++
         *************** Beginning of data
****************************************
0001.00    A        R ITEMMSTR                 TEXT('VENDORP  DB
FORMAT')
0002.00    A          VNDNBR      5S 0         COLHDG('VENDOR' 'NUMBER')
0003.00    A                                   ALIAS(VENDOR_NUMBER)
0004.00    A          ITNO        6S 0         COLHDG('ITEM' 'NUMBER')
0005.00    A          ITDESC      25           COLHDG('ITEM
DESCRIPTION')
0006.00    A                                   ALIAS(ITEM_DESCRIPTION)
         ****************** End of data
********************************************



 F3=Exit   F5=Refresh   F9=Retrieve  F10=Cursor   F11=Toggle   F12=Cancel
 F16=Repeat find         F24=More keys
                               (C) COPYRIGHT IBM CORP. 1981, 2000.
```

Logical Files

The AS/400 and IBM I systems also use an object type called a logical file. Logical files are created by programmers using DDS just as physical files. The big difference between logical files and physical files is that logical files do not contain data. With internally managed indices, they point to specific records of physical files. Only physical files can contain data, but when you query a logical file, you will most certainly believe that it has data. It doesn't. But, it does provide a nice funnel through which the data passes to your query.

Logical files can be used for many things. They are a very powerful tool for application developers. For example, you can use a logical file to re-sequence the VENDORP file data by say, vendor number. You can also create logical files to show only a portion of a physical file. For example, you may not want certain users to see certain records. Additionally, you may not want certain users to see certain fields of data. The Query user cannot tell the difference when using a logical file.

Logicals Do the Join for which they don't need Query

Logical files can also be used to combine or join the data in two different files. For example, the VENDORP file and the ITEMP files could be combined by a programmer to form a joined logical file. If a programmer had created one of these for us, we would not need Chapter 19 in this book. Instead of joining the files in the Query/400 definition, as we do in Chapter 19, we could have selected the joined logical file and designed the query as if it were using one file.

Performance Impact of Logical Files

When programmers are nice enough to build logical files, it sure makes Query use substantially easier. However, in all fairness to your IT staff, logical files do place a performance burden on the system and some systems may perform poorly if many logical files are used. If your IT ream does not give you logical files to use, it may be that overall performance can suffer.

What Is in the Database?

The AS/400 database consists of file objects (logical and physical) An object contains a set of rules as to how the object can be used as the code (methods) to provide the function. Along with all that, the file object holds the contents (data) of the object if the object is a file. The file object also contains lots of data about the file object itself, such as the person who created the file, the date created, the number of records, and the fields that are defined within the object. The file object even stores the field prompts that are used in your queries. Yes, if you find that your prompts are not very good, you should ask your IT team to make them better.

Let's look at three commands so that we can get a better feel for the database. After all, if we have no database, we can have no queries.

Looking At Database Objects

The file object VENDORP was created in the HELLO library. To
see the contents of the file without doing a query, you can type the
display physical file member command (DSPPFM). By the way,
members are file sub-objects in which separate sets of data for the
same file can be stored. Most files have just one member. If a file
has data, it has at least one member to store the data. The DSPPFM
command is as follows:

DSPPFM HELLO/VENDORP

Press ENTER and you will see the following panel in Figure A-3:

Figure A-3 Display Data First Fifteen Records

```
                         Display Physical File Member
File . . . . . . :    VENDORP           Library . . . . :    HELLO
Member . . . . . :    VENDORP           Record . . . . . :    1
Control . . . . .                       Column . . . . . :    1
Find . . . . . . .
*...+....1....+....2....+....3....+....4....+....5....+....6....+....7....+...
00038J B COMPANY             3817 N. PULASKI        SCRANTON      PA &   A
00040SCRANTON INC            2147 S MAIN ST         OLD FORGE     PA Î   A
00042PASS PAX INC            1539 OAK HILL          OLD FORGE     PA Ê   A
00044J B EQUIP INC           2232 FOUEST            SCRANTON      PA &   A
00046K D BUTTS WALLACE INC   2150 TOUGHY            SCRANTON      PA &   A
00048DENTON AND BALL         7934 S SCRANTON AVE    SCRANTON      PA &|  A
00049JOHN STUDIOS            2040 N BELTWAY         SCRANTON      PA &¬  A
00025A MACHINE CORP.         1345 Prill Avenue      Chicago       ILá□   A
00026B MACHINERY             45 Ginzo Lane          Wokegon       OK Á"  A
00028C ENGRAVING CO          Pedulllion Avenue      Greghert      ILáo   A
00030D CONTROLS              45 Fognetta Place      Kernstin      ILá`   A
00032I POWER EQUIPMENT       56 Fineel La           Swingder      PA &   A
00034ROBIN  COMPANY          11 Robin Lane          Robin         PA ø   A
00036F STEEL CO              78 Engraved Rd.        Mattusic      PA ß±  A
00052Bird Bath House         39 Seedy Lane          Tena Hoopit   PA ß   A
                                                                     More...
  F3=Exit    F12=Cancel    F19=Left    F20=Right    F24=More keys
```

Displaying Physical File Data

In Figure A-3, as you can see, the VENDORP records are listed in
the sequence that they exist in the database. That's called arrival
sequence. The order they got into the file is the order in which they
are shown. The first 78 characters of the VENDORP record are there
for your perusal in the first window. To see more data for the same
records, press F20 to scroll right. Let's not do that now. Instead, let's
roll down to see the last two records of the file. Press the Page down
or Roll down key one time and you will be taken to the panel in
Figure A-4.

Figure A-4 Display Data - 16, 17 Records

```
                       Display Physical File Member
File . . . . . . :     VENDORP          Library . . . . :     HELLO
Member . . . . . :     VENDORP          Record . . . . . :     16
Control . . . . .                       Column . . . . . :     1
Find . . . . . . .
*...+....1....+....2....+....3....+....4....+....5....+....6....+....7....+...
00056Feenala Grund Mfg.       765 Neophite Blvd        Castigoga      MIic    A
00010Thinking Clocks           43 Timestamp Rd         Gottime        GA      A
                       ****** END OF DATA ******

                                                                       Bottom
F3=Exit    F12=Cancel    F19=Left    F20=Right    F24=More keys
```

Displaying Hexadecimal Data

As you can see, just the last two records are shown in Figure A-4. Take a look at the right side of these records in position 73 to 75. Notice the garbage over on the right. That's because the field which follows STATE is of packed decimal format. That should mean about nothing to you at this point. But, remember, some of your data will be in this condition when you do your own queries.

Packed decimal uses both halves of a storage position (byte). It sticks its numbers in both halves, rather than putting the number in half and the sign in the other. Sometimes programmers like to see what is in both halves of a byte to look at the contents of specific data positions in a disk file.

To do this, you press the F10 key to display hexadecimal. You then get a panel which would look like mostly garbage. From there, without thinking, press the F11 key to see the both halves of the byte (one on top of the other) on top of each other with the numbers visible. When you hit those keys in that sequence, you will be taken to a panel that looks like Figure A-5 below.

Figure A-5 Display Data - Hexadecimal

```
                    Display Physical File Member
File . . . . . . :    VENDORP          Library . . . . :    HELLO
Member . . . . . :    VENDORP          Record . . . . . :    16
Control . . . . .                      Column . . . . . :    1
Find . . . . . . :
*...+....1....+....2....+....3....+....4....+....5....+....6....+....7....+...
00056Feenala Grund Mfg.       765 Neophite Blvd      Castigoga      MIic    A
FFFFFC8898984C9A984D8844444444FFF4D89988A84C9A844444444C8AA88988444444DC58100C
00056655513107945404 67B00000007650556 78935023540000000003123976710000004953F2F1

00010Thinking Clocks          43 Timestamp Rd        Gottime        GA      A
FFFFFE88998984C9989A4444444444FF4E898AA8994D84444444444C9AA89844444444CC03100C
000103895295703363220000000000043039452314709400000000007633945000000007192F3F1

                        ****** END OF DATA ******

                                                                      Bottom
F10=Display character    F11=Display side by side    F24=More keys
```

The Halves

For your convenience, we have blown up the both halves of storage positions 73 through 75, of both records, below. One half of a storage position is on top of the other. Read from top left to bottom right.

581 = **55831**
53F

031 = **09321**
92F

In Figure A-5 (and immediately above), you can see the values over on the right side after the state abbreviations. The first record has 55831F. This means 55831 with a plus sign. The second record has 09321F, and this means 09321 with a plus for a sign. Now, let's look at the object itself ,so that we can see what field starts in position 73 of the record immediately following the state abbreviation.

Look at Record Layout in File Object

To do this, we can use the Display File Field Description command (DSPFFD) against the VENDORP file. However, since the programmer used the VENDORPA reference file to create this file origincally, the more concise information for learning is stored in VENDORPA. To look inside this object to see the record layout, type the following:

DSPFFD HELLO/VENDORPA

Press ENTER, and you will see the panel in Figure A-6.

Figure A-6 Check The VENDORP Record Layout DSPFFD

```
                        Display Spooled File
File  . . . . . :    QPDSPFFD                  Page/Line    1/41
Control . . . . .                              Columns     1    78
Find  . . . . . .
*...+....1....+....2....+....3....+....4....+....5....+....6....+....7....+..
     Coded Character Set Identifier  . . . . . :    37
  CITY        CHAR        15      15      56        Both     CITY
     Field text . . . . . . . . . . . . . . :  CITY
     Coded Character Set Identifier  . . . . . :    37
  STATE       CHAR         2       2      71        Both     STATE
     Field text  . . . . . . . . . . . . . :  STATE
     Coded Character Set Identifier  . . . . . :    37
  ZIPCD       PACKED       5  0     3      73        Both     ZIP'CODE
     Field text  . . . . . . . . . . . . . :  ZIP CODE
     Alternative name  . . . . . . . . . . . :  ZIP_CODE
  VNDCLS      PACKED       2  0     2      76        Both     VENDOR
                                                             CLASS
     Field text  . . . . . . . . . . . . . :  VENDOR CLASS
     Alternative name  . . . . . . . . . . . :  VENDOR_CLASS
  VNDSTS      CHAR         1       1      78        Both     ACTIVE
                                                             CODE
                                                              More...
 F3=Exit   F12=Cancel   F19=Left   F20=Right   F24=More keys
```

Well, looky here! We found the ZIPCD (zip code field) at position 73 right after the state abbreviation. To store the 5 digits of zip code, notice that the file takes just 3 positions of disk space. This is why programmers pack data. It saves disk space. However, this saving often makes it more difficult for Query users..

It is important to re-emphasize that we just dipped into a file object to get this information. The best place to store a record layout is in the file object. Yes, it is also in VENDORP, but there is about a screen-worth of information about each field, since the object wants to report about the reference file that was used when the object was created. We don't need all that for this.

Checking Out ITEMP's Record Layout

Before we move on, let's also look at the ITEMP file which was also created with a reference file. In this case, we will look at the file, not the dictionary. You can see that there is lots more information than you want. To do this type the following:

DSPFD HELLO/ITEMP

Press ENTER and roll down twice. You will be taken to Figure A-7.

Figure A-7 Check The ITEMP Record Layout DSPFFD

```
                        Display Spooled File
File  . . . . . :   QPDSPFFD                 Page/Line   1/42
Control . . . . .                            Columns     1    78
Find  . . . . . .
*...+....1....+....2....+....3....+....4....+....5....+....6....+....7....+..
.
              Data      Field  Buffer    Buffer      Field   Column
     Field    Type      Length Length  Position      Usage   Heading
     ITNO     ZONED       6  0      6         6       Both    ITEM
                                                             NUMBER
       Field text . . . . . . . . . . . . . . :  ITEM NUMBER
       Referenced information
         Referenced file . . . . . . . . . . . :  ITEMPA
           Library . . . . . . . . . . . . . . :  HELLO
         Referenced record format  . . . . . . :  ITEMMSTR
         Referenced field  . . . . . . . . . . :  ITNO
         Attributes changed  . . . . . . . . . :  None
              Data      Field  Buffer    Buffer      Field   Column
     Field    Type      Length Length  Position      Usage   Heading
     ITDESC   CHAR        25     25        12         Both    ITEM
DESCRIP
       Field text . . . . . . . . . . . . . . :  ITEM DESCRIPTION
       Referenced information

More...
F3=Exit   F12=Cancel   F19=Left   F20=Right   F24=More keys
```

Lots of Reference Information - Clutter

Notice all the reference information about the fields. There are only three fields in this file as you can see in the DDS in Figure A-2. The last two fields (ITNO and ITDESC) are highlighted in the above panel, to call them to your attention.

Looking at File Descriptions

Now, let's look at some other information in this database file object. To display a file description, you use the display file description command (DSPFD). Notice there is just one "F."

DSPFD HELLO/VENDORP

Figure A-8 Display File Description VENDORP

```
                        Display Spooled File
File  . . . . . :    QPDSPFD                 Page/Line   2/2
Control . . . . .                            Columns     1   78
Find  . . . . . .
*...+....1....+....2....+....3....+....4....+....5....+....6....+....7....+..
.
   Access path . . . . . . . . . . . . . . . :        Arrival
   Sort Sequence . . . . . . . . . . . . . . : SRTSEQ  *HEX
   Language identifier . . . . . . . . . . . : LANGID  ENU
 Member Description
   Member  . . . . . . . . . . . . . . . . . : MBR     VENDORP
     Member level identifier . . . . . . . . :         1020505173632
     Member creation date  . . . . . . . . . :         05/05/02
     Text 'description'  . . . . . . . . . . : TEXT    Vendor Master
 File
     Expiration date for member  . . . . . . : EXPDATE *NONE
     Member size                               SIZE
       Initial number of records . . . . . . :             10000
       Increment number of records  . . . . . :         1000
       Maximum number of increments  . . . . :         3
     Current number of increments  . . . . . :               0
     Record capacity . . . . . . . . . . . . :             13000
     Current number of records . . . . . . . :                17

More...
 F3=Exit    F12=Cancel    F19=Left    F20=Right    F24=More keys
```

The File Object Reports

In the panel in Figure A-8, the most important piece of information is very near the bottom. There are 17 records in the file. Who told us this? The file object did it! This data is not in some big directory someplace. The file itself reported this information to the display when we asked.

When Were You Used Last?

For our next trick, lets find out when this file was last used. No, we're not going to go ask everybody that might have used it. That was in the olden days. The system now keeps track of this information within the objects themselves. Dear File Object ...

WRKOBJD / DSPOBJD

We do this by using the work with objects command (WRKOBJ) as follows:

WRKOBJ HELLO/VENDORP

Press ENTER, followed by option 8 on the object line, and you will get the following panel as in Figure A-9.

Figure A-9 Display Object Description from WRKOBJ

```
                  Display Object Description   Full
                                                    Library 1 of
1
Object . . . . . . . :    VENDORP      Attribute . . . . . :   PF
  Library . . . . . :      HELLO       Owner . . . . . . . :   DEBS
Type . . . . . . . . :    *FILE        Primary group . . . :   *NONE

User defined information:
  Attribute . . . . . . . . . . . :
  Text . . . . . . . . . . . . . . :    Vendor Master File

Creation information:
  Creation date/time . . . . . . . :    05/05/02  17:36:31
  Created by user . . . . . . . . :     BKELLY
  System created on . . . . . . . :     HELLO
  Object domain . . . . . . . . . :     *SYSTEM




More...
Press Enter to continue.

F3=Exit   F12=Cancel
(C) COPYRIGHT IBM CORP. 1980, 2000.
```

Who Did What to Whom?

You can notice in Figure A-9 that Brian Kelly (me) created the file on 5/5/2002 after 5:00 P.M. Hmm! I must have been working O.T.?

But, the object has not reported when it was used last. Well, maybe it has. See the "More" in the bottom right of the panel? The operating system has all of it in memory waiting for you to get it. To get to the rest of the information, hit the roll or page down key and you will see the top section of the panel in Figure A-10.

Figure A-10 WRKOBJ - Last 3 Panels

```
                        Display Object Description    Full
                                                          Library 1 of
1
Object . . . . . . . :    VENDORP        Attribute . . . . . :    PF
  Library . . . . . :      HELLO         Owner . . . . . . . :    DEBS
Type . . . . . . . . :    *FILE          Primary group . . . :    *NONE

Change/Usage information:
  Change date/time . . . . . . . . :    09/03/02  15:30:27
  Usage data collected . . . . . . :    YES
  Last used date . . . . . . . . . :    09/18/02
  Days used count  . . . . . . . . :    22
    Reset date . . . . . . . . . . :
  Allow change by program  . . . . :    YES
Auditing/Integrity information:
  Object auditing value  . . . . . :    *NONE
  Digitally signed . . . . . . . . :    NO


       ------------------------------------------------------

More...

  Storage information:
    Size . . . . . . . . . . . . . . . :    36864
    Offline size . . . . . . . . . . . :    20480
    Freed  . . . . . . . . . . . . . . :    NO
    Compressed . . . . . . . . . . . . :    INELIGIBLE
    Auxiliary storage pool . . . . . . :    1
      Object overflowed  . . . . . . . :    NO
  Journaling information:
    Currently journaled  . . . . . . . :    NO
------------------------------------      ------------------

More...

  Save/Restore information:
    Save date/time . . . . . . . . . . :    08/18/02  07:37:54
    Restore date/time  . . . . . . . . :
    Save command . . . . . . . . . . . :    SAVLIB
    Device type  . . . . . . . . . . . :    Tape
    Sequence number  . . . . . . . . . :    171
    Volumes  . . . . . . . . . . . . . :    TAP001
    File label ID  . . . . . . . . . . :    HELLO
    Save format  . . . . . . . . . . . :    Serial


Bottom
Press Enter to continue.

F3=Exit    F12=Cancel
```

Lots of Information to Give

The last day this file was used was 9/17/2002 and it was used 22 times since it was created. After the first "More," I pasted the two other parts to the display object panels above. The middle shows size information, and the last panel snippet above the bottom shows when the object was saved last. Looks like it needs to be saved again, eh?

That's a lot of information to store about an object. Hopefully, this little section will help you get more familiar with the idea of a database so that your queries can be even more meaningful.

The Things We Learned About Database!

Remember all that we learned in this little Appendix

1.   Programmers use DDS to create database file objects such as VENDORP.

2.   Files can be physical or logical.

3.   Only Physical files contain data.

4.   Logical Files pretend to hold data since they are as usable in a Query as a physical file.

5.   All file objects exists in libraries.

6.   One or more file objects can be called a database.

7.   A file member holds the records in a file (17 records in VENDORP).

8.   A record is a group of related fields (Joe's record)

9.   A file is a group of related records (Payroll file)

10.   A field is a fact in a record (Joe's pay)

11.   Data is/are unorganized facts

12.   Information is data organized to facilitiate decision making.

11.   The DSPPFM command lets you look inside the front part of the contents of a database file to see the data.

12.   The DSPFD lets you look inside the file to find specific information about the file such as its allocation size, and the current number of records.

13.   The DSPFFD gives you a field list (record layout) of the file.

14   The WRKOBJ permits you to find a file; display it and gain information about who created it; when was it last used, etc.

15.   Your Queries can work against both physical and logical files.

16.   When you want to know what something really is, ask the great folks in IT.

17.   Many data elements in files have strange formats, including packed decimal. Some are not Query friendly. When you encounter these in your Queries, ask your friendly IT team to tell you what it means and how you can work with such data.

Downloading the Exercise Database Files

For this Book, feel free to go to the www.letsgopublish.com web site. Look for the Pocket Query Guide downloads and bring them down. Since the site is reasonably old, and the book uses stuff that is old, if you have trouble reaching us, send an email to books@letsgopublish.com or to publisher@ kellyconsulting.com. We'll certainly try to get them to you but of course for a book originally written in 2002 for a product set (IBM i) that is still used and mostly unchanged, the stuff may be gone. IT Jungle may be able to help. They are the best source of IBM I information on the planet.

LETS GO PUBLISH! Books by Brian Kelly: (Sold at www.bookhawkers.com; Amazon.com, and Kindle.).

LETS GO PUBLISH! is proud to announce that more AS/400 and Power i books are becoming available to help you inexpensively address your AS/400 and Power i education and training needs: Our general titles precede specific AS/400 and other technology books. Check out these great patriotic books which precede the tech books in the list.

Seniors, Social Security & the Minimum Wage
The impact of the minimum wage on Social Security Beneficiaries

How to Write Your First Book and Publish It With CreateSpace
This books teaches how to create a book with MSWord and then publish it with CreateSpace. No need to find a traditional publisher.

Healthcare & Welfare Accountability The Trump Way
Why should somebody win the Lottery & not pay back welfare?

The Trump Plan Solves Student Debt Crisis. .
This is the Trump solution for new student debt and the existing $1.3 Trillion student debt accumulation.

Take the Train to Myrtle Beach The Trump Way.
Tells all about the Donald Trump Plan to restart private passenger railway systems in America while it tells you how to get to Myrtle Beach by Train.

RRRRRR The Trump Way.
This book represents the overarching theme of the Trump campaign with verbs ready to reign in the excessive policies of the Obama Administration. These are the six verbs for the RRRRRR plan: Reduce, Repeal, Reindustrialize, Raise, Revitalize, Remember

Jobs! Jobs! Jobs! The Trump Way!
All about the jobs mess we ae in along with a set of Trump solutions

The Trump Plan Solves the Student Debt Crisis
Solution for new student debt and the existing $1.3 Trillion debt accumulation

101 Secrets How to be a High Information Voter
You do not have to be a low-information voter.

Why Trump?
You Already Know… But, this book will tell you anyway

Saving America The Trump Way!
A book that tells you how President Donald Trump will help America sn that Americans wind up on top

The US Immigration Fix
It's all in here. Finally an answer to the 60 million interlopers in America. You won't want to put this book down

I had a Dream IBM Could be #1 Again
The title is self-explanatory

Whatever Happened to the IBM AS /400?
The question is answered in this new book.

Great Moments in Penn State Football Check out the particulars of this great book at bookhawkers.com.

Great Moments in Notre Dame Football Check out the particulars of this great book at bookhawkers.com or www.notredamebooks.com

WineDiets.Com Presents The Wine Diet Learn how to lose weight while having fun. Four specific diets and some great anecdotes fill this book with fun and the opportunity to lose weight in the process.

Wilkes-Barre, PA; Return to Glory Wilkes-Barre City's return to glory begins with dreams and ideas. Along with plans and actions, this equals leadership.

The Lifetime Guest Plan. This is a plan which if deployed today would immediately solve the problem of 60 million illegal aliens in the United States.

Geoffrey Parsons' Epoch... The Land of Fair Play Better than the original. The greatest re-mastering of the greatest book ever written on American Civics. It was built for all Americans as the best govt. design in the history of the world.

The Bill of Rights 4 Dummmies! This is the best book to learn about your rights. Be the first, to have a "Rights Fest" on your block. You will win for sure!

Sol Bloom's Epoch ...Story of the Constitution This work by Sol Bloom was written to commemorate the Sesquicentennial celebration of the Constitution. It has been remastered by Lets Go Publish! – An excellent read!

The Constitution 4 Dummmies! This is the best book to learn about the Constitution. Learn all about the fundamental laws of America.

America for Dummmies!
All Americans should read to learn about this great country.

Just Say No to Chris Christie for President two editions – I & II
Discusses the reasons why Chris Christie is a poor choice for US President

The Federalist Papers by Hamilton, Jay, Madison w/ intro by Brian Kelly
Complete unabridged, easier to read version of the original Federalist Papers

Companion to Federalist Papers by Hamilton, Jay, Madison w/ intro by Brian Kelly
This small, inexpensive book will help you navigate the Federalist Papers

Kill the Republican Party! (2013 edition and edition #2)
Demonstrates why the Republican Party must be abandoned by conservatives

Bring On the American Party!
Demonstrates how conservatives can be free from the party of wimps by starting its own national party called the American Party.

No Amnesty! No Way!
In addition to describing the issue in detail, this book also offers a real solution.

Saving America
This how-to book is about saving our country using strong mercantilist principles. These same principles that helped the country from its founding.

RRR:
A unique plan for economic recovery and job creation

Kill the EPA
The EPA seems to hate mankind and love nature. They are also making it tough for asthmatics to breathe and for those with malaria to live. It's time they go.

Obama's Seven Deadly Sins.
In the Obama Presidency, there are many concerns about the long-term prospects and sustainability of the country. We examine each of the President's seven deadliest sins in detail, offering warnings and a number of solutions. Be careful. Book may nudge you to move to Canada or Europe.

Taxation Without Representation Second Edition
At the time of the Boston Tea Party, there was no representation. Now, there is no representation again but there are "representatives."

Healthcare Accountability
Who should pay for your healthcare? Whose healthcare should you pay for? Is it a lifetime free ride on others or should those once in need of help have to pay it back when their lives improve?

Jobs! Jobs! Jobs!
Where have all the American Jobs gone and how can we get them back?

Other IBM I Technical Books

The All Everything Operating System:
Story about IBM's finest operating system; its facilities; how it came to be.

The All-Everything Machine
Story about IBM's finest computer server.

Chip Wars
The story of ongoing wars between Intel and AMD and upcoming wars between Intel and IBM. Book may cause you to buy / sell somebody's stock.

Can the AS/400 Survive IBM?
Exciting book about the AS/400 in a System i5 World.

The IBM i Pocket SQL Guide.
Complete Pocket Guide to SQL as implemented on System i5. A must have for SQL developers new to System i5. It is very compact yet very comprehensive and it is example driven. Written in a part tutorial and part reference style, Tons of SQL coding samples, from the simple to the sublime.

The IBM i Pocket Query Guide. (This book)
If you have been spending money for years educating your Query users, and you find you are still spending, or you've given up, this book is right for you. This one QuikCourse covers all Query options.

The IBM I Pocket RPG & RPG IV Guide.
Comprehensive RPG & RPGIV Textbook -- Over 900 pages. This is the one RPG book to have if you are not having more than one. All areas of the language covered smartly in a convenient sized book Annotated PowerPoint's available for self-study (extra fee for self-study package)

The IBM I RPG Tutorial and Lab Guide – Recently Revised.
Your guide to a hands-on Lab experience. Contains CD with Lab exercises and PowerPoint's. Great companion to the above textbook or can be used as a standalone for student Labs or tutorial purposes

The AS/400 & IBM i Pocket Developers' Guide.
Comprehensive Pocket Guide to all of the AS/400 and System i5 development tools - DFU, SDA, etc. You'll also get a big bonus with chapters on Architecture, Work Management, and Subfile Coding. This book was updated in 2016..

The IBM i Pocket Database Guide.
Complete Pocket Guide to System i5 integrated relational database (DB2/400) – physical and logical files and DB operations - Union, Projection, Join, etc. Written in a part tutorial and part reference style. Tons of DDS coding samples.

Getting Started with The WebSphere Development Studio Client for System i5 (WDSc). Focus is on client server and the Web. Includes CODE/400, VisualAge RPG, CGI, WebFacing, and WebSphere Studio. Case study continues from the Interactive Book.

The System i5 Pocket WebFacing Primer.
This book gets you started immediately with WebFacing. A sample case study is used as the basis for a conversion to WebFacing. Interactive 5250 application is WebFaced in a case study form before your eyes.

Getting Started with WebSphere Express Server for IBM i Step-by-Step Guide for Setting up Express Servers
A comprehensive guide to setting up and using WebSphere Express. It is filled with examples, and structured in a tutorial fashion for easy learning.

The WebFacing Application Design & Development Guide:
Step by Step Guide to designing green screen IBM i apps for the Web. Both a systems design guide and a developers guide. Book helps you understand how to design and develop Web applications using regular RPG or COBOL programs.

The System i5 Express Web Implementer's Guide. Your one stop guide to ordering, installing, fixing, configuring, and using WebSphere Express, Apache, WebFacing, System i5 Access for Web, and HATS/LE.

Joomla! Technical Books

Best Damn Joomla Tutorial Ever
Learn Joomla! By example.

Best Damn Joomla Intranet Tutorial Ever
This book is the only book that shows you how to use Joomla on a corporate intranet.

Best Damn Joomla Template Tutorial Ever
This book teaches you step-by step how to work with templates in Joomla!

Best Damn Joomla Installation Guide Ever
Teaches you how to install Joomla! On all major platforms besides IBM i.

Best Damn Blueprint for Building Your Own Corporate Intranet.
This excellent timeless book helps you design a corporate intranet for any platform while using Joomla as its basis.
4
IBM i PHP & MySQL Installation & Operations Guide
How to install and operate Joomla! on the IBM i Platform

IBM i PHP & MySQL Programmers Guide
How to write SQL programs for IBM i

Joomla! books and many of the tech books above are only available at www.bookhawkers.com